FAITH,
REASON, AND HISTORY

FAITH, REASON, AND HISTORY

Rethinking Kierkegaard's *Philosophical Fragments*

by

Robert C. Roberts

MERCER

The paper used in this publication meets
the minimum requirements of American National Standard
for Information Sciences—Permanence of Paper
for Printed Library Materials, ANSI Z39.48-1984.

Library of Congress Cataloging-in-Publication Data

Roberts, Robert Campbell, 1942-
Faith, reason, and history.

Includes index.
1. Kierkegaard, Soren, 1813-1855. Philosophiske
smuler. 2. Religion—Philosophy. I. Title.
BL51.K4873R63   1986   201   86-18182
ISBN 0-86554-228-7 (alk. paper)

CONTENTS

PREFACE

THIS BOOK has been simmering for eight or nine years now, most of the time on some back burner. It is humbling to think that it has taken me all this time (and the task is not finished) to rethink a book that Kierkegaard penned in a few months, working part-time. I do not remember ever having *set out* to write it, though by the time I had written about fifty pages, I began to suspect that it was coming on. It was drawn from me, almost without my consent, out of the fascination and exasperation I experienced as I read and reread Kierkegaard's seductive pamphlet. It was not always on a back burner, of course, and was mostly written during some sabbatical months in 1980 that I had intended to spend on another project. For the sabbatical I am grateful to have been supported by Western Kentucky University, the Institute for Ecumenical and Cultural Research (Collegeville, Minnesota), and the Institute for Advanced Christian Studies. Wheaton College, where I now teach, has provided financial support for the publication of this book. I am also thankful to my friend Richard Olmsted, a pastor in the United Church of Christ, for the many hours he spent with me discussing thoughts of Johannes Climacus in the basement of the library at St. John's University. Another friend, C. Stephen Evans of St. Olaf College, has greatly influenced my thinking about *Philosophical Fragments*,[1] causing me to rethink my rethinking at a number of points. I dedicate this book to my little buddy Nathan, who at the age of seven already shows a proclivity for climbing.

---

[1]The translation upon which my book is based is that of Howard Hong and Edna Hong (Princeton: Princeton University Press, 1985).

INTRODUCTION

WHAT THIS BOOK IS LIKE

THIS BOOK IS AN EXPERIMENT in reading Kierkegaard. I say "in reading Kierkegaard," rather than "in Kierkegaard scholarship," because Kierkegaard intended his books to be *read* in a sense different from that in which great books like his are consumed in the course of doing scholarship on them. It is symptomatic of Kierkegaard scholarship that it eventuates in books with titles like *Kierkegaard's Thought, Kierkegaard's Relation to Hegel, Time and the Self in Kierkegaard's Pseudonymous Works,* and even just *Kierkegaard;* and in essays with titles like "Kierkegaard's Dialectic of Existence," "The Loss of the World in Kierkegaard's Ethics," and "A Critique of Kierkegaard's Doctrine of Subjectivity." In such scholarly writings one finds attempts to give systematic overviews and defenses or critiques of Kierkegaard's "doctrines" about various matters, to characterize his thought in general, to place it in the historical and intellectual context of his day, to relate it to the history of philosophy, and sometimes to show how his writings are the results of his personal crises and psychological maladjustment.

In proposing to experiment with another way of reading Kierkegaard, I do not suggest that the scholarly approach to him is without value (I have indulged in a bit of it myself, from time to time); it is indeed at least as valuable as any other scholarship, and probably more valuable than most, since its objects (Kierkegaard's person and thoughts) are so intensely interesting and personally instructive.

There is, however, a touch of irony in calling the approach of the present book experimental, as though I were doing something innovative or even perhaps on the borders of intellectual respectability, since I am proposing to read Kierkegaard as he intended to be read. Whatever the values of scholarship may be, Kierkegaard regarded with horror the prospect that he and his works would become the objects of it. He did not want to be systematized, defended by disciples, compared with Hegel and Kant and Plato, or explained in terms of his environment and psychological makeup. Instead, he wanted to be read "primitively," by particular individuals for their own use, who would find in his reflection an occasion for their own reflection about the issues of human existence. He wanted a reader who would painstakingly rethink the issues after him, stimulated by Kierkegaard's (or his pseudonyms') thoughts and by the incitement of the dialectical knots they strewed on the pathways of their pages. Like Socrates, Kierkegaard did what he could to avoid engendering disciples, and tried instead to engender clarity and rigor and honesty of thought and heart in his reader.

Louis Mackey, sensitive to the violence that Kierkegaard has suffered at the hands of scholars who wish to turn him into a straightforward theorist of some sort, says

> Kierkegaard's writings are storehouses of philosophical and theological materials, and it is only prudent that modern philosophers and theologians should go into Egypt to replenish their own barns. . . . But the fact is that if Kierkegaard is to be understood *as Kierkegaard,* he must be studied not merely or principally with the instruments of philosophic and theological analysis, but also and chiefly with the tools of literary criticism.[1]

It is hard to believe that Kierkegaard would be any happier with Mackey's approach, especially if it is successful, than he would be with that of the philosophers and theologians Mackey chides. For Kierkegaard, especially in his pseudonymous writings but also more generally, precisely does not want "to be understood *as Kierkegaard.*" He wants, instead, to be a dispensable vehicle for his reader's coming to understand *other* things.

The present book is an experiment in honoring Kierkegaard's desire to be read in a more primitive way. It takes seriously Johannes Climacus's asseverations that *Philosophical Fragments* is not "doctrinizing," but is ironical and an instance of indirect communication. It will, accordingly, take the text of *Fragments* primarily not as a primary object of inquiry, but as a stimulus to thought about the issues that the text addresses. One, cannot, of course, entirely circumvent inquiry about the text, for the text is sometimes difficult and one needs to have some idea what it means if it is to be allowed to do its maieutic work. Moreover, part of the maieutic work gets accomplished precisely in the process of untangling the text's possible meaning.

My reading of *Fragments* is an experiment in yet another sense. My attitude toward the words of Johannes Climacus is modeled by Climacus himself in the attitude he takes, in the *Concluding Unscientific Postscript,* towards some sayings of Gotthold Lessing.

> The considerations which will be brought forward under this head and the following, are more definitely referrible to Lessing, in so far as there are utterances of his which may be quoted directly. But yet again, not with any simple certainty; for Lessing is not dogmatic but subjectively evasive, showing no wish to pledge anyone to the acceptance of his view for his sake, and in

---

[1]Louis Mackey, *Kierkegaard: A Kind of Poet* (Philadelphia: University of Pennsylvania Press, 1971) x (Mackey's italics).

no way seeking to help others establish a direct relationship in continuity with him. It is possible that Lessing has understood that such things cannot be communicated directly; at any rate his procedure can be explained in this manner, and the explanation is possibly the right one: I say only possibly.[2]

Climacus is as "subjectively evasive" as his Lessing, and so I shall treat him with the experimental tentativeness and personal independence that befits reading such an ironical author.

Just as *Fragments* is a thought experiment, so is my reading of it: Sometimes when I ascribe to its author one view or another, I shall bracket my statement with an explicit "possibly." In reality even when I speak, for stylistic felicity, in the categorical mood, my reading should be bracketed by this "only possibly." I shall occasionally, unironically, tell you what I believe about sense perception or love or necessity or Jesus. But as an interpretation of Johannes Climacus, this book is experiment pure. I shall be guided by the text(s) and by whatever dialectical ingenuity I possess; but with an author like Climacus, to go further and draw a positive conclusion about his views would be a breach of etiquette that I could not forgive myself.

Kierkegaard's writings are devoted to a corrective task, that of reintroducing Christianity to Christendom. The situation in which he proposed to be a Socrates for the sake of Christian teaching was one, like that of the original Socrates, in which illusion had first to be dispelled. In Kierkegaard's case, the illusion was that people are Christians—people whose vocabulary is Christian but whose concepts are roughly Hegelian, who discuss Christianity volubly but whose passions, emotions, and practice are left unshaped by Christian thoughts, who subtly defend themselves against the inroads of God's Spirit by evaluating themselves solely with reference to the social herd in which they dwell. In such a situation it would be ineffectual to address people directly with simple Christian truths, say those of Luther's *Shorter Catechism.*

So Kierkegaard's task was to write a devious literature that would seduce his reader to abandon the illusions of "Christendom," and then, bereft of them and naked, to confront God in his holiness and mercy. Part of his method of drawing the reader into this web of personally significant reflection is to cause a certain fecund confusion in his reader's mind: "so long as I live it is part of my task to employ about two-thirds of my strength in confusing, in working against myself and weakening the impression."[3] In effecting this means to a higher end, he has perhaps succeeded too well; the

[2]Johannes Climacus, *Concluding Unscientific Postscript,* trans. David Swenson and Walter Lowrie (Princeton: Princeton University Press, 1941) 86.

[3]From a Preface to *Christian Discourses,* not originally published; see *Christian Discourses,* trans. Walter Lowrie (New York: Oxford University Press, 1961) 2.

confusions that were intended to be passing episodes in the reading lives of
Kierkegaard's contemporaries have seized whole generations and communities of scholars. Possibly he would not be dismayed at this. Perhaps we
professors have got what we deserve. Our hearts have been revealed; having
loved the darkness, we now have wandered so deep into the cave that there
is no escape for us. Charity to the professors, however, is also charity to
Kierkegaard. Even toward professors Kierkegaard cannot have been so cold-
hearted.

Am I not patronizing the great author if I try to give readers a more
straightforward access to his (possible) thought by pointing out where the
irony may lie? Stricken by a similar doubt, O. K. Bouwsma half-apologizes
at the start of his comments on Wittgenstein's *Blue Book:*

> if I understand [*The Blue Book*], and there are some readers who do not, per-
> haps I can help them to understand it, or at least help them not to misunder-
> stand in certain ways or help them to misunderstand it in a certain preferred
> way. This is rather strange since it seems to involve that the author himself
> failed to help them to understand it or failed to help them enough, and so some
> reader comes forward to do what the author did not do. In some cases this
> seems to be how it is. Think of all the helps over hard places for boys and men
> in reading Kant, for instance, supplied by helpers. Very well, then, I too am a
> little helper. But if I am such a little helper I am going to help myself gener-
> ously to the helpmost helper, namely, the author himself. I will help the reader
> to the help offered by the author, reminding the reader of those helps.[4]

In what follows I propose to be one of Kierkegaard's little helpers. I shall explain in unpedantic detail what he does not explain, to help the boys and
girls, as well as the women and men, over some of the difficult places.

In addition to explaining what Kierkegaard does not explain, I shall, like
Bouwsma, help the reader to the help offered by our author. The very fact
that Kierkegaard himself supplies such help, and supplies it in abundance,
is an answer to a third objection to my experimental project: that if Kierkegaard's method of communicating the truth depends on deceiving his
reader, then the necessary result of my straightening the reader out (even
if only experimentally) is that I deprive him of access to that truth. The existence of a book like *The Point of View for My Work as an Author* and of the
many passages in Kierkegaard's works and journals in which he explains his
irony, show that explanation of irony does not, in his view, deprive it of its
force. It is, of course, ideal that the deceived reader begin to suspect on his
own that he is being had, follow up that hypothesis, and then unravel the
deception for himself. But where the ideal cannot be attained, irony still re-
tains some power.

---

[4]"The Blue Book," in *Philosophical Essays* by O. K. Bouwsma (Lincoln: University
of Nebraska Press, 1965) 177.

FRAGMENTS AS INDIRECT COMMUNICATION

That *Fragments* is in some sense a work of irony is manifest even to a quick reading. The author, Johannes Climacus of Copenhagen, admits to being "a loafer out of indolence," and seems to exult in the fact that his social utility approximates that of Archimedes, who sat "undisturbed, contemplating his circles while Syracuse was being occupied" (5). This self-depreciation, however, like that of entitling his book *Fragments* in an age when all real philosophers were striving heroically after the holistic ideal, is in fact a satire upon the busyness and self-importance of his age.

Not only is Climacus an idler with no opinion about the matters discussed in his book (see 7). The formal project of the book is outrageous. It is a thought-experiment in which, starting with one assumption, he deduces all the pivotal concepts of Christian dogmatics. An interlocutor comes on stage at the end of each chapter, and a dialogue ensues. In the first two chapters, Climacus, hanging his head in mock shame, admits to an odd plagiarism, and also admits by implication that the deduction has been a piece of sophistry: He did not deduce the positions from his hypothesis, after all, but got them from the Bible.

If there is a serious purpose to these chapters (and, as I shall try to show, to the whole book), it cannot be the establishment of its conclusions on the basis of a process of reasoning. This, of course, is not to say that whatever purpose the book does have could be accomplished apart from the processes of reasoning through which the reader is led. If the purpose of the book were entirely independent of its reasonings, it would not be ironical; it would just be a misfire. The success of the book, if it be successful, is testimony that reflection is good for more than conclusion-drawing. Certain thought-processes might be, as Plato thought, a procedure for personal transformation;[5] or as Wittgenstein thought, a means of seeing the world aright.[6] Who knows, they might even be a means of spiritual awakening.

That the point of the book is not to establish one or another truth, Climacus makes abundantly clear with the scorn he pours upon a certain German professor who published a review of the book in a theology journal. The professor included an abstract, about which Climacus says

> The abstract is accurate, and as a whole dialectically reliable, but here is the point: in spite of the accuracy of the abstract, everyone who reads that only is bound to get an entirely false impression of the book. The abstract is doctrinizing, pure and unadulterated doctrination; the reader will get the impres-

---

[5]See *Republic,* bks. 6-7.

[6]Ludwig Wittgenstein, *Tractatus Logico-Philosophicus,* trans. D. F. Pears and B. F. McGuinness (London: Routledge & Kegan Paul) 6:54.

sion that the book is also doctrinizing. Now this is in my view the most distorted impression of the book it is possible to have. The contrast of the form; the challenging opposition between the experiment and the content; the impudence of the invention (which even invents Christianity), the only attempt made to go beyond, namely, beyond the so-called speculative construction; the unwearied incessant activity of the irony; the parody on speculative philosophy involved in the entire plan of the work; the satirical in making exertions as if *"was ganz Ausserordentliches und zwar Neues"* were to issue, and then coming out with nothing but old fashioned orthodoxy in a suitable degree of severity: of all this the reader of the review gets not the slightest intimation.[7]

The poor professor does indeed glimpse the irony in the book, for he ends his review by leaving it to the judgment of each reader to decide whether he will look for seriousness or irony in this "apologetic dialectic." To end a review of so manifestly ironical a book with this kind of comment, says Climacus, is to satirize oneself. The professor becomes a victim of Climacus's irony rather than its beneficiary because he does not follow the scent he momentarily sniffs.

In a book written about five years later by another pseudonym, Kierkegaard has this to say about "indirect communication":

It can be produced by the art of reduplicating the communication. This art consists in reducing oneself, the communicator, to nobody, something purely objective, and then incessantly composing qualitative opposites into a unity. This is what some of the pseudonyms are accustomed to call "double reflection." An example of such indirect communication is, so to compose jest and earnest that the composition is a dialectical knot—and with this to be nobody. If anyone is to profit by this sort of communication, he must himself undo the knot for himself.[8]

Philosophical Fragments is such a "dialectical knot," a tangled composition of jest and earnest. To understand it—"to profit by this sort of communication"—the reader must do what the German professor does not do. He must take cognizance of the dissonances in the work, and resolve them. "He must himself undo the knot for himself." In this work I want to do just this, to read *Fragments* as a knot of spoof and Christian seriousness to allow its "dialectic" to have the effect it was meant to have. By this means I shall try to let Kierkegaard be my teacher, not only by his presenting truths to me, but by his presenting me something else that occasions my becoming my own teacher, my "reduplicating" in my person what he possibly has achieved in his own. So he will, in a sense, disappear. It goes without saying that if I

---

[7]Climacus, *Concluding Unscientific Postscript,* 245n.

[8]*Training in Christianity,* trans. Walter Lowrie (Princeton: Princeton University Press, 1944) 132.

am to remain to you, my reader, in the humble role of little helper that I have assigned myself (little helper to a much bigger, but still little, helper), I too must disappear. My procedure will be to point out incongruities in some detail and attempt to resolve them.

Perhaps I should say just a word here about my method of sorting out the jest from the seriousness. There are, of course, the more or less obvious clues provided by the author. I have already mentioned the dialogues at the ends of the chapters and the remarks that are to be found in the *Postscript*. In particular, the remark about "the contrast of the form" is suggestive, for the "form" of *Fragments* is that of a deductive thought-experiment, and so we should be especially on the lookout for irony in those aspects of the book that are parts of the deduction. If we are to understand the book in its details, however, we will need a more particularized sorting method than this kind of indication affords us. Climacus wants us to think critically as we untie his knot, and not to think only about his text, as if it were some kind of puzzle that he had produced to titillate our love of ingenuity; he wants us to reflect on the issues that he addresses.

Accordingly, a chief criterion will be whether what is said stands up to critical scrutiny. If it stands up, I shall tend to take it seriously; if not, this fact will incline me to relegate it to the jest-pile. This is only natural and right. By using this criterion I am not claiming that the historical Climacus would countenance all the critical devices I use in evaluating his arguments. I am being true to his spirit, however, for he desires by his subtle therapy to lead us, not to understand him, but to understand ourselves in relation to Jesus Christ. Though I think my judgments about Climacus's intentions are for the most part correct, I would be far less dismayed to find out that I had misunderstood him than to find out that I had misunderstood the issue that he is discussing. For Climacus's method of indirect communication, not only is it essentially irrelevant what the author of the communication intended; it is positively counterproductive to be overly serious about ferreting out his intention as such. "Precisely in the degree to which I understand a thinker I become indifferent to his reality; that is, to his existence as a particular individual, to his having realized his teaching, and so forth."[9] Only the truth is of paramount importance, and I shall try in what follows to keep my priorities straight. Thus, my role as little helper is not so much to help my reader understand Climacus (much less Kierkegaard), as to help him read the book.

Before we take up the details of analysis, there is one more preliminary that may be worth exploring.

---

[9]Climacus, *Concluding Unscientific Postscript*, 289.

A NOTE ABOUT THE AUTHOR

The title page of *Fragments* reads, "by Johannes Climacus." S. Kierke-gaard is "responsible for publication." We have a biographical sketch of this Johannes, and perhaps we should not miss the opportunity to gain insight into the cast of his ideas by learning something of his personality.

His biographer tells us that he lived, as entirely as a human being can, in a world of thought and imagination. He gets his name, "the climber," because he, like Hegel, climbs up to heaven by his syllogisms.[10] His namesake, a Byzantine monk of the seventh and eighth centuries, wrote a treatise entitled *Scala Paradisi* containing advice to monks for attaining spiritual perfection.[11] Our latter-day Climacus had a different kind of ladder:

> It was his delight to begin with a single thought and then, by way of coherent thinking, to climb step by step to a higher one, because to him coherent thinking was a *scala paradisi* [ladder of paradise], and his blessedness seemed to him even more glorious than the angels'. Therefore, when he arrived at the higher thought, it was an indescribable joy, a passionate pleasure, for him to plunge headfirst down into the same coherent thoughts until he reached the point from which he had proceeded. Yet this did not always turn out according to his desire. If he did not get just as many pushes as there were links in the coherent thinking, he became despondent, for then the movement was imperfect. Then he would begin all over again. If he was successful, he would be thrilled, could not sleep for joy, and for hours would continue making the same movement, for this up-and-down and down-and-up of thought was an unparalleled joy.[12]

As we begin to wend through *Philosophical Fragments,* we will see a mind at work that fits well this description. Readers of this book have not sufficiently appreciated its ladder-like structure. I shall show how the first half of the book (chapters 1-3) is a continuous deductive argument in which Climacus climbs up and "impudently," as he himself says, enters the heavens by "inventing" Christianity with nothing more substantial to go on than a simple hypothesis and a fancy for inferences. Only the first half of the book is a ladder, however, for it makes sense that once he reaches the heights he quits climbing and does some exploring (chapters 4-5). As we might expect with a project like Climacus's, we will sometimes be distressed on his be-

---

[10]See *Søren Kierkegaard's Journals and Papers,* ed. and trans. Howard Hong and Edna Hong (Bloomington: Indiana University Press, 1967-1978) vol. 2, #1575.

[11]See Niels Thulstrup's commentary printed in *Philosophical Fragments,* trans. David F. Swenson and rev. Howard V. Hong (Princeton: Princeton University Press, 1962) 148.

[12]*Johannes Climacus,* printed in the same volume as *Philosophical Fragments,* trans. Howard Hong and Edna Hong (Princeton: Princeton University Press, 1985) 118.

half; but even then, our exploration of the ladder may indirectly teach us some things about Christianity.

It might be thought that from the Climackean authorship of *Fragments* we not only get clued on certain forms of fishiness in thought that may help us to begin unraveling the irony, but we get a wholesale solution: nothing in the book is Kierkegaard's; it is all irony. The book is pseudonymous, and after all Kierkegaard himself has said that "in the pseudonymous works there is not a single word which is mine."[13]

Short-circuiting the dialectic in this way would be a total mistake. It is of no interest whatsoever to know that "the whole book" is ironical, whatever that might mean; the irony can have its therapeutic effect only upon someone who descends to the details and works them out. Further, we are not intellectual biographers—or, insofar as we are, we have left off learning from Kierkegaard's irony and have started delving into his private life. Preventing the reader from taking such a detour is precisely Kierkegaard's major avowed reason for creating the pseudonyms. If anybody, says he, "has perverted for himself the impression of the pseudonymous books by an ill-conceived intrusion upon my factual personality . . . then this surely is not my fault, who becomingly and in the interest of the purity of the relationship have for my part decidedly done all that I could to prevent what a curious portion of the reading world (God knows in the interest of whom) has done everything to attain."[14] It would, of course, be just as perverting if we took a gossipy interest in "what Johannes Climacus really believed." It is difficult to arouse much enthusiasm for that project; Johannes does not have enough solidity to be the object of interesting gossip. We will not get diverted into his intellectual biography, but can stick to the business of sorting out his irony, because with him we have only the "light ideality of a poetically actual author to dance with."[15]

Does not Kierkegaard egotistically exaggerate his personality's power to divert his reader away from self-knowledge, and seduce him to curious researches into the author's mind? Evidently not. Despite his pleas and ploys for anonymity, there is a veritable scholarly industry devoted to probing his life for clues to his authorship. One of the fruits of this probing is our knowledge that *Philosophical Fragments* originally had a different title page and preface from the ones that were finally published with it, and that in the original S. Kierkegaard is named as author. Niels Thulstrup concludes: "In-

---

[13]"First and Last Declaration," in the second paragraph, printed following *Concluding Unscientific Postscript.*

[14]Ibid.

[15]Ibid.

asmuch as Søren Kierkegaard is the author, according to the draft of the title-page, this can only mean that the work represents his own views."[16]
Kierkegaard's later explanations of the purpose of the work as ironical and
indirect communication are, accordingly, benign rationalizations. I will leave
it to my reader's judgment, after he has followed my ruminations through
the arguments of the book, to decide whether it is remotely plausible that
the book represents Kierkegaard's own views in such a way as not to require
interpretation as a work of indirect communication. At any rate, it does not
follow from Kierkegaard's signing his name to a work as its author, that the
work is not ironical. The pamphlets and newspaper articles with which he
attacked the religious establishment are as full of irony as anything he wrote.
Admittedly, the irony there is not as sustained or as dark as it is in *Fragments*. Indeed, if my interpretation is correct, it is probable that nowhere in
Kierkegaard's writings is the irony as unwearied, incessant, dark, and masterful as it is in this book.

THE FORM AND CONTENT OF *FRAGMENTS*

Let me now give an anticipatory survey of the content and form of *Philosophical Fragments*. This section of comments will be fully understandable
only in the context of the details of the rest of this book; but it may nevertheless be useful at this point to have a quick overview.

Fragments' teachings, insofar as they can be put in direct discourse, reduce to a few theses that, from the point of view of Christian orthodoxy, ought
to be noncontroversial:

   (1) The relationship that an individual can sustain to Jesus Christ is cate-
       gorically different from that which he or she can have to any merely hu-
       man teacher.
   (2) The relationship between Jesus Christ and his disciple is initiated by
       God's loving and sacrificial act of becoming a man.
   (3) The affirmation that Jesus of Nazareth is the Lord of the universe, while
       it is the most important and life-transforming affirmation that the dis-
       ciple makes, cannot be warranted by any of the normal canons of his-
       torical reasoning, and even contradicts some broadly held canons of
       historical reasoning.
   (4) Anyone who comes into a genuine relationship with Jesus Christ trav-
       erses the possibility of offense.

---

[16]In his commentary, 146.

(5) With respect to the difficulty of coming into a genuine relationship with him,[17] there is no essential difference between any later disciple of Christ and the disciples who were historically contemporary with him.

As to the form of *Fragments* the title page sets the general problem: How is it possible to base an eternal happiness on a historical point of departure? The first three chapters do not address this question head-on, however, but are an elaborate preparation for that discussion, which takes place in chapters four and five.

The first three chapters develop the consequences of the hypothesis of a "teacher" whose identity and person, by contrast with the case of Socrates, are essential to his "teaching" activity. In the first chapter the deduction establishes that the disciple must be in a state of sin, the teaching must take the form of the re-creation or rebirth of the disciple, and the "teacher" must be the god. The second chapter establishes that the teacher is motivated by love for the disciple, that his purpose is to establish a love-relationship with the disciple, and that he can perform this act of teaching only by becoming incarnate as a human suffering servant. The third chapter asks what attitude the potential disciple (here often called the "understanding") takes to the teacher's enterprise, and Climacus deduces that the disciple's attitude is ambivalent: he or she longs for such a teacher but at the same time is repulsed by him, seeing him as the absolute paradox, a stumbling block to Jews and folly to Greeks.

---

[17]Louis Mackey is the interpreter of Kierkegaard who, to my knowledge, has best understood the ironical character of *Fragments.* But his attempt to sum up the positive thrust of the book is incredible. "What Climacus is getting at . . . is that the historicity of human life screws every truth, Greek or Christian, into a paradox, since truth is timeless and the truth-seeker temporal. . . . Climacus forces his reader into a corner where he must admit—not that the Christian hypothesis is true, for that 'is an entirely different question, which cannot be decided in the same breath'—but that there is no honest way of understanding human existence that can avoid contradiction. . . . The final battle is pitched between the essentialist philosopher who views life under the aspect of eternity and the existential thinker who grapples daily with the paradoxes of his life and surmounts them in recollection or in faith." (*Kierkegaard: A Kind of Poet,* 164-65) Mackey's words would be much better as a characterization of any number of Kierkegaard's other works, e.g., *Fear and Trembling, The Sickness Unto Death,* the *Postscript* (especially 177ff.). Throughout his literature Kierkegaard tries to make his reader aware of the possibilities of a deeper existence, and this existence, whether Socratic or Christian, involves anxieties and sufferings (what Mackey calls "contradictions") with which more superficial forms of existence are unacquainted. As a description of what is peculiar to *Fragments,* Mackey's characterization flagrantly ignores the fact that every chapter of the book is devoted to a discussion of the relationship between Christ and his disciple, and that the discussion of the Socratic viewpoint is always subservient to this, as an illuminating contrast.

Having established these points by the deductive activities of the first three chapters, Climacus is now ready for a more descriptive account of faith, which is a historical judgment[18] that is the basis for an eternal happiness. Chapter four describes faith in the case of people who are historically contemporary with the appearance of the god as a human suffering servant; chapter five describes it in the case of later generations who must rely for this historical knowledge upon testimonies. Sandwiched between chapters four and five (ostensibly to give the impression of the passage of exactly 1,843 years) is the Interlude, a highly abstract and didactic general discussion of the nature of historical events and of judgments about them.

---

[18]Or, to speak more precisely, a judgment concerning the identity of a historical person.

PART ONE

CLIMBING

CHAPTER 1

THOUGHT-PROJECT

TEACHERS

CLIMACUS BEGINS WITH A PANEGYRIC upon Socrates, whose moral and intellectual grandeur are due to the "wonderful consistency" with which he held fast his basic insight about the limits of a teacher's role in a pupil's life. His conception of that role is humble: the particular identity of the teacher is indifferent to the pupil *qua* pupil. (It is, of course, not necessarily indifferent to the pupil *qua* friend, spouse, son, and so forth.) The pupil's learning does not become sound because it was *this* teacher who introduced it to him.

Since the learning has to sit on its own bottom and can only with a terrible confusion be thought to gain support from the authority of the teacher, all discipleship, so loved by professional teachers, is out. By "discipleship" we mean that attitude, on the learner's part, in which he thinks the truth of his learning is necessarily conditioned by its source in his teacher. The only true discipleship, if one wants to call it that, is one in which the pupil takes an attitude of "forgetfulness" about the historical occasion of his learning (that is, the concrete person of his teacher), and the teacher, for his part, humbly recognizes his dispensability. Socrates expressed this humility in the avowal that he was only a midwife, a vanishing occasional helper as the laboring learner gave birth to his *own* ideas.

Let us introduce a few distinctions to draw more precisely the limits of Socrates' insight. It surely is not entirely due to confusion that teachers have been honored and paid, and particular individuals sought for what they could teach. If teachers are only occasions for their pupils' learning, they are occasions in various ways that ought to be specified. One of Socrates' more favored contexts is that of mathematical learning and teaching. A great mathematician like Euclid or Russell or Gödel who makes some discovery is certainly in some sense in a privileged position for making the discovery. His privilege takes primarily the form of an extraordinary talent for mathematics, the hard work that it takes to bring this talent to flower, and a certain propitious placement in the history of mathematical thought. Given these conditions, (1) it still remains true that the discovery in question might have been made by other people (and sometimes a discovery is in fact made by more than one person). (2) Once the discovery has been made, however, the discoverer can teach it only by way of inducing others to "see through" the mathematical relations for themselves, that is, to reduplicate, in some sense, the original discovery. The discoverer can at best only guide others in this process; he cannot deliver the mathematical truth to them the way that an eyewitness of some historical occurrence can authoritatively deliver some historical truths. So obviously, (3) it is inappropriate for a pupil to appeal to his teacher's authority in support of the soundness of his mathematical reasoning.

Another teaching context is that of historical facts. Like a mathematician who by his brilliance, hard work, and the accidents of his circumstances is in a peculiarly good position to make some discovery, particular individuals are sometimes privileged for the knowing of historical truths. James Boswell, for example, had privileged access to certain truths about Samuel Johnson. As such, he is an authority on some things that Johnson thought and did in a way that nobody can be an authority on a mathematical truth: For some facts about Johnson, such as some things that Johnson did and said during their tour of the Hebrides, his testimony is the court of last appeal. So there is a disanalogy with (3) and (2) above: It is sometimes appropriate, in historical matters, to appeal to the authority of a peculiarly circumstanced witness, and a person can be said to know the truth in question on that basis, and without having gone through anything like the process of acquiring it that the witness did. The analogy with (1) holds: It did not have to be Boswell who is our source for this truth; it might well have been somebody else. So even though Boswell happens to be the authority for some things that we know about Johnson, it is appropriate for him to maintain Socratic humility about his role as teacher; it is only by the accidents of history that he has this privileged position.

Yet another context is that of religious knowledge. Here is an example of a religious truth: If a person ascribes his sufferings to God's disciplinary grace, he will begin to take joy in them. This is an insight that is not likely to occur to most people, who if they ascribed their sufferings to God's agency at all, would probably be disposed to see in them an alienation from his grace rather than a manifestation of it. Yet there does not seem to be anything intrinsically impossible about a person's coming to see his sufferings in this way simply by meditating on various ways of combining the ideas. A person who had come to this insight in a heartfelt way might become a teacher of it. The analogy with mathematical learning is more perfect here than it is with historical learning. If a learner acquires this insight from a teacher, there is certainly no necessity that it be *this* teacher; and it is conceivable that the learner has learned it without recourse to any teacher at all. If the learner is to learn the truth in a heartfelt way (and what other way is there to know

such a truth?), he will do so only by establishing his own corresponding relationship with God and any appeal to the authority of the teacher will be a
misunderstanding of the kind of truth here in question. If the teacher's purpose is achieved, the teacher will have been dispensed with.[1]

AN AMAZING DEDUCTION

The purpose of Climacus's ruminations about the grammar of teacher-
pupil relations is to prepare us for the assumption on which he bases his
thought experiment. This assumption is, in Climacus's words, that "the moment in time must have . . . decisive significance" (13).[2] This notion has two
elements. First, it suggests a teacher-pupil relation in which, by contrast with
the Socratic situation, the identity of the human teacher is essential to the
pupil's learning. That is, the follower can learn what he learns only from this
teacher, who thus stands to him in a relation of authority. Second, it suggests that the knowledge that the pupil gains in this relationship depends
on his sustaining his relationship with the teacher. Socrates can teach and
then be on his way, and the pupil is none the worse for Socrates' departure;
but if the teacher whose identity is essential to his teaching takes leave of
the disciple, he necessarily deprives the pupil of the knowledge he imparts.

Climacus does not just assume that the teacher's identity and presence
is essential to his teaching activity, but places this assumption in an assumed context. When he speaks about the "truth" that the teacher is to teach,
he is speaking of a religious and ethical truth, the state of being a "true" or
genuine human being. This is the sort of truth that Socrates was centrally

---

[1] It is perhaps partly because of these analogies between religious and mathematical insights that both have sometimes been called "eternal," in contrast with
historical truths. I say partly, because by these criteria the laws of physics and bi-
ology, which have not usually been called eternal truths, would be too.

[2] Climacus uses the word "moment" (øieblik) in three different ways without
alerting his reader. In the phrase quoted above, the sense seems to be, (1) "the time
of the teacher's historical appearance." Thus Climacus later names it "the fullness
of time" (18). Sometimes "moment" is used (2) to designate the teacher himself. Thus
"whether or not [the pupil] is to go any further, the moment must decide" (20). And
(3) sometimes the word is used to designate the time in the learner's life when he
becomes discipled to the teacher: "In *the moment,* a person becomes aware that he
was born" (21). (Note that he does not say that in the moment the learner is *born,*
but that in the moment the follower becomes *aware* that he was born.) From the
nature of the thought project that is being conducted on its basis, it seems clear that
(2) is the primary sense, with (1) a corollary of this; (3) derives its distinctiveness
entirely from (2) and (1); that is, if the identity of the teacher, and consequently his
historical individuality, are not decisive for the learner's status as learner, then the
moment in the learner's life in which he comes into contact with the teacher can
have no features different from the moment of learning from a Socrates.

interested in teaching: "In the Socratic view, every human being is himself the midpoint, and the whole world focuses only on him because his self-knowledge is God-knowledge" (11). Thus we are talking about a teacher who teaches "human virtue," to use Socrates' expression (see *Apology*), a teacher whose teaching activity aims at transforming not just the content of a person's mind or the state of a person's mental skills, but the person himself at his "heart." The "knowledge" that is aimed at here is the knowledge of the good, and it is knowledge in the deepest sense possible: To know the good in this sense is to be good. It is to love and obey God, to be unwavering in one's commitment to truth and honesty, to be courageous and just and loyal to one's friends, and to have integrity in all this (purity of heart).

What follows, concerning the nature of the pupil, the identity of the teacher, and the nature of the learning relation, from Climacus's assumption?

First, says Climacus, it follows that the pupil not only is not in possession of the truth; he is not even in a condition to acquire it. If he were, then we would be back in the Socratic situation. He is, of course, the sort of being for whom it is appropriate that he should possess the truth; for the truth is the fulfillment of his nature. If, as it is assumed, the learner cannot learn the truth apart from this particular teacher's presence with him, then it follows that this teacher must supply something to him that only this teacher can supply, and that is a necessary condition for his learning the truth. His condition has to be something in which the pupil is entirely lacking apart from the teacher; for if he had a little of the condition, then he might be able to start on his journey towards the truth without the teacher, or in such a way that the teacher was a dispensable occasion for his setting out on the journey.

From this it follows, says Climacus, that anyone who is to become a learner must be re-*created* by the teacher. Of course, not every conferral of a condition for coming into possession of some truth would have to amount to the re-creation of the person upon whom the condition is conferred. For example, if the truth in question is a biographical truth about Samuel Johnson, Boswell might be entirely lacking the condition for knowing that truth unless Johnson confers it upon him, and Johnson might confer it upon him by inviting him to spend the day with him. This example, however, does not deal in the kind of truth that Climacus assumes in his hypothesis. The "truth" in question here is an ethical and religious one, the fulfillment of the pupil's being as human. So that if the pupil does not have this truth, he is, in a sense, not himself. Likewise, the condition is a condition for the pupil's being himself. So it seems plausible that a person could receive the condition for knowing this truth only from his creator. If someone is a creator of human beings, he must be the god. So it follows that the hypothetical teacher is the god.

How did the learner come to lack the condition for understanding the truth? The answer is easy, according to Climacus, because there are only three candidates, and two of them involve contradictions:

> This [deprivation] cannot have been due to an act of the god (for this is a contradiction) or to an accident (for it is a contradiction that something inferior would be able to vanquish something superior); it must therefore have been due to [the learner] himself. .... But this state—to be untruth and to be that through one's own fault—what can we call it? Let us call it *sin*. (15)

Let us begin by examining the premises.

Why could we not charge the god with depriving man of the condition for knowing the truth? We have already established that the god, if he is to become a teacher of the truth, creates in the pupil the condition for possessing it. The truth is defined as the fulfillment of the nature that the pupil was originally created to realize. So if the god were to deprive the pupil of the condition, he would be depriving him of the condition to realize the nature for the realization of which he created him. This would set the god at contradictory purposes with himself.

Why is it not possible that humans lost the condition through an accident? Climacus avers that for that to have happened would be for the inferior to have overcome the superior, which is a "contradiction." Now it is not generally true that the inferior cannot overcome the superior. Stupid hoodlums and even accidents have been known to kill important dignitaries. Again we must interpret "superior" and "inferior" in terms of Climacus's context. The "superior" is human moral and religious perfection. (That is what Climacus means by "truth.") Climacus means that there is something conceptually odd ("contradictory") in the notion that somebody lost the condition of his moral and religious perfection in any other way than by *acting* wrongly, morally and religiously. In the *Apology* Socrates avers that the eternal law forbids a better man to be hurt by a worse, and he means that it is inconceivable that one person should be caused by another to lose his virtue. There is only one person in the world who can lose your virtue for you, and that is you. (So this argument could be used also against the supposition that the god deprived people of the condition: Even the god does not have the power to make a person immoral.) Similarly, if I do what appears to be an immoral act by "accident," through ignorance or faulty equipment or some such thing, then by the very fact that it was an accident that caused me to do the wrong, my wrong is not a violation of my virtue. Thus it is contradictory to suppose that the inferior could overcome the superior.

So unless we can think of a fourth way that persons might have lost the condition for knowing the truth, it seems to follow that they lost it by their own responsible act—that is, the moral spoiling of human nature came into the world, and comes into every individual who is spoiled, through a responsible act. If it comes any other way, it is not the moral spoiling of human nature, and the individual, however corrupt he may outwardly seem, is still in his innocence.

The learner cannot get himself out of this state; if he could, the second part of our assumption would be vitiated. For if, upon noticing his state of untruth, the learner could simply mend his ways and thereby regain the condition for understanding the truth in question, the teacher would be, like Socrates, dispensable. Therefore the learner is not just in sin, but in *bondage* to sin, and the teacher, in consequence, can be called *savior* and *deliverer*. Since the bondage has the character of guilt, the release from it must be effected by an *atonement* (reconciliation). The teacher's bestowing the condition on the learner is a trust, for which the learner will be held accountable in the future, especially in a future life. So the teacher can be called *judge*. Since the teacher recreates the learner, the event of teaching can be called the *new creation*. Since the learner in his former state was constantly in the act of departing from the truth, his new state must be the result of *conversion*. If the learner is to be turned away from a state of guilt, he must be aware of it; but to be aware of guilt is to sorrow, and so the change will have the character of *repentance*.

So it seems that, from the assumption of a religious teacher whose identity and presence are essential to his teaching activity, Climacus has deduced basic Christianity. Has he? Certainly all the terms are central terms of Christian theology, and he refers in the *Postscript* to "the impudence of the invention (which even invents Christianity)." He has not, of course, deduced that the teacher-god must become incarnate as a human being (that work is left to the next chapter), nor that he must be a folly and a stumbling block to worldly ways of thinking (that he leaves for chapter three), and nowhere in the book does he go so far as to deduce that the god's name must be Jesus and that he must have grown up in Nazareth, and so forth. But the pretension is clearly to have deduced the idea of Christianity, a historical religion, from a simple assumption. We have seen that he has done a surprisingly good job, if one grants all the dimensions of the assumption.[3]

At the end of chapter one, however, Climacus confronts an imaginary accuser:

[You] are behaving like a vagabond who charges a fee for showing an area

---

[3] I owe my appreciation of the strength of Climacus's argument to my friend Steve Evans, who persuaded me to grant Climacus a richer assumption than I was earlier inclined to do.

that everyone can see. You are like the man who in the afternoon exhibited for a fee a ram that in the forenoon anyone could see free of charge, grazing in the open pasture. (21)

That is: You, Climacus, pretend to have deduced Christianity from the hypothesis that the moment has decisive significance, when it obviously exists in the world, there for everybody to see. What a ridiculous project, to invent something that already exists. Climacus hides his head in mock shame, and the discussion that ensues makes it clear that the deduction has been a deceit. Climacus really got the idea of Christianity from the Bible or his mother or somewhere else, but certainly not by deducing it from the hypothesis.

This accusation incites Climacus to reflect on the question of who *did* invent Christianity. He then presents a premise to the conclusion that no one could have invented Christianity, and from this it follows that only God could have invented it. But if God did invent it, then it is true: "Yet this oddity enthralls me exceedingly, for it tests the correctness of the hypothesis and demonstrates it" (22). Let me raise two questions about this claim. First, what does Climacus mean by claiming that the hypothesis has been "demonstrated"? Second, does the consideration that Climacus presents prove that the hypothesis is true?

It has seemed to some readers that Climacus cannot be talking about the truth of Christianity, since to do so would be to abandon the hypothetical nature of his thought project. After all, in the Moral Climacus says,

> This project indisputably goes beyond the Socratic, as is apparent at every point. Whether it is therefore more *true* than the Socratic is an *altogether different question,* one that cannot be decided in the same breath. (110; my italics)

Thus C. Stephen Evans says, "Climacus means, I think, that his hypothesis has been proven to be correctly formed; i.e., it is a genuine alternative to Socrates."[4] There are at least three reasons for thinking this interpretation wrong. First, for a thinker of Climacus's caliber, his forming a hypothesis correctly is not an "oddity" that is likely to "enthrall [him] exceedingly"; it ought to be something he is used to. Second, the "oddity" that demonstrates the hypothesis is "that something like this *exists,* about which everyone who knows it also knows that he has not invented it" (22, my emphasis). It is not the object of the hypothesis *as hypothesized* that is so strange, but that it exists—that the hypothetical "teacher"-claim exists in history. Third, what demonstrates the hypothesis is that "it would indeed be unreasonable to require a person to find out all by himself that he does not exist" (22). The

---

[4]*Kierkegaard's* Fragments *and* Postscript (Atlantic Highlands NJ: Humanities Press, 1983) 32 n. 12.

assumption of this *reductio* is that somebody has discovered that he does (did) not exist. No one discovers that he does not exist merely by forming a hypothesis that, *if* it turned out to be true, *would* imply that he did not exist.

So the "correctness" of the hypothesis to which Climacus refers is not just the correctness of its formation, but the objectivity of its reference—that there exists such a "teacher" as the hypothesis deduces. Odd as it may seem, Climacus has stepped out of the role of hypothesizer and taken up that of someone who knows the historical existence of Christianity. But really his stepping (partially) out of the role of ironist here is not as odd as it may seem, for he has already stepped out of it in admitting that the deduction was a deceit.[5]

Let us now consider the argument that supposedly proves the truth of Christianity. This is how it goes:

> Nobody can have invented Christianity, since anyone who did so would be in the position of discovering of his own accord that he does not exist,[6] which is absurd. But since Christianity exists and no human being invented it, then God must have invented it. But if God invented it, then it is true.

In chapter one Climacus seems to have outlined, using just his imagination and capacity for contrast, a religion at least very similar to Christianity. Ob-

---

[5]There remains, of course, the tension between Climacus's "demonstration" of the truth of Christianity and the Moral, which maintains strictly the hypothetical character of *Fragments* with respect to the truth of Christianity (or the Christianity-like religion of the hypothesis). But the tension between the "demonstration" and the Moral is no more problematic than the general tension between the deceit of the hypothesis and the serious intent of Climacus's project. How the "demonstration" fits together with Climacus's broad views on the relations between arguments and faith is yet another question, upon which some light may be thrown when we get to the discussion of *Fragments,* ch. 3.

[6]Of course no biblical writer actually says that prior to their salvation people do not exist, nor that in coming to reckon with their salvation and accept it, they acknowledge that apart from their salvation they were nonexistent. What at least one biblical writer does say is that prior to their salvation his readers were dead—in their "trespasses and sins" (see Ephesians 2:1-10). They were not just sickly or weak or ignorant or out of touch with their human potential or in some other way *deficient* in "truth"; they were dead. The implication, of course, is that restoration to being in the "truth" could be accomplished by nothing short of an act of God: they needed to be born again, made into a new creation. It is the absolute desperation of the human plight apart from the non-Socratic teacher that both Climacus and the apostle are getting at with their talk of death and nonexistence.

The "demonstration" to which Climacus refers goes something like this: if anybody is so deeply mired in "untruth" that the only cure for him is a resurrection, then it is inconceivable that he should conceive without God's help what his plight is. Thus, if we have a conception of our being in such a plight, the conception must derive from God and consequently be veridical.

viously he already knew Christianity and was guided in his "deduction" by this knowledge. So he did not, as a matter of fact, invent Christianity or this religion that is so similar to it. But *might* he have done so?

Admittedly, it seems psychologically improbable that an individual, in ignorance of Christianity, would come up with the religion that Climacus outlines. Climacus seems to argue that inventing this religion is impossible because it would imply the absurd situation that the inventor discovered of his own accord that he did not exist. This seems to be incorrect, however, since the inventor would not have to believe the religion (indeed, knowing that he had invented it would seem to be good grounds for not believing it), and if he did not believe it he could hardly be said to have "discovered" the truth of any of its doctrines. If a person did devise on his own a religion according to which he was dead in the sense in which Christianity claims that people are dead, there would seem to be something problematic about his then going on and believing it, since that is the kind of belief that is believed, if at all, only on authority. If the inventor kept his judgment in suspension, as Climacus does, there would seem to be nothing absurd about the position.

Furthermore, it does not seem impossible that a religion analogous to Christianity be both invented and believed by its inventors, provided that the inventors are not aware of their inventing activity. This is the sort of picture of the development of Christianity offered by the history of religions school: the doctrines and practices gradually evolved by purely human and historical causes, without the "inventors" being aware of what they were doing.

This having been said, however, it does seem to me that pondering the origins of Christianity can produce a strong impression of its truth. It certainly was not invented by any individual, and appeared too suddenly complete in its essentials to have evolved in the manner the history of religions school suggests. Moreover it is at the same time so humanly profound and so strange to human ears that Paul's description of it in the words of Isaiah,

> What no eye has seen, nor ear heard,
> nor the heart of man conceived,
> What God has prepared for those who love him,

seems perfectly fitting.

JESUS AND SOCRATES

Climacus's serious purpose is not to produce valid deductions, but to point out some pertinent incompatibilities. His real, as opposed to ostensible, program is to begin with the historically given basic Christian understanding of Christ and to compare it with another paradigm of religious teaching. The Socratic paradigm is of interest because it is one in terms of which theologians and philosophers, as well as ordinary people, are strongly and perennially inclined to think of Christ—with the result that their Christianity is fundamentally distorted. The Christ-disciple relationship has some grammatical features that are incompatible with some features characterizing any relationship between a merely human religious teacher and his "disciple." It is Climacus's purpose to impress[7] these incompatibilities upon his reader. The point of Climacus's discourse, then, is to force upon his reader some fundamental exclusive disjunctions ("either/or's") that will inoculate him against a certain kind of heretical understanding of Jesus and thus free him to come into the correct kind of relationship with Christ.

As a set of documents in the history of ideas, the New Testament has the remarkable feature of being at the same time utterly preoccupied with a single individual, a carpenter-preacher from the town of Nazareth who flourished in the early years of the first century, and about the salvation of human persons.[8] The message, summed up, is that this man's death is the uniquely necessary condition for the salvation of the world, and that individuals can become beneficiaries of this salvation by confessing this crucified one, who is alive at the right hand of God, as their Lord. Nobody else's death could work salvation, because this man alone is the Lord of the universe. Since this man is Lord, any analogous attachment of discipleship to any other human being could only be idolatry and the very opposite of salvation.

Now let us compare the disciple's clinging for dear life to this crucified one with the relation an individual might have with a Socratic religious teacher. We will call this latter the SRT for short. There are as many possible messages of SRTs as there are natural religious ways of construing the world, but let us take as our example again the SRT whose message is that if a person ascribes his sufferings to God's disciplinary grace, he will find joy in them. So our SRT seeks, by various means, to bring his "disciple" to a visceral understanding of this truth about joy in suffering. That is, he seeks to bring it

---

[7]I use the word "impress" advisedly: he is interested not just in *making* these distinctions, as a philosopher might be, in a purely inquisitive mood. He is interested in *communicating* them, in making them unavoidable for his reader, as a preacher might be, in an evangelistic mood.

[8]Yet the preoccupation with this individual is not a biographical one. The Gospels are concerned to give us enough details of his teaching and his actions to indicate the basis and character of his claim to be Lord, but they seem not to be very concerned with giving a chronological account and are nearly silent about Jesus' formative years. Paul and others do not speak even of the details of his ministry, mentioning for the most part just his death and resurrection. There is something fitting about the lack of biographical interest and detail here, for there is really just one important thing about Jesus' identity, and when *it* is adequately indicated, further detail becomes a way of missing the point: this man is the Lord and the lamb of God.

about that his disciple takes joy in his sufferings by virtue of this thought, for that is the only way to have a religious understanding of this truth. The various means may include (1) telling the "disciple" this truth, (2) exemplifying the truth in the teacher's own person or telling him edifying stories about persons who have exemplified it, (3) leading the disciple, by "questioning," around to a fuller conceptual grasp of the truth in question, so that he begins to get for himself a perspicuous view of the conceptual and psychological context of the truth.

Since the joy, which is the point of the SRT's teaching, is a *God*-relationship, the SRT will have failed to the extent that his pupil's mind and heart are filled with his relationship to the SRT. The SRT will have succeeded in his teaching mission only if the pupil learns to count his relationship with his teacher as incidental to the truth in question, and finds his joy in God alone. No doubt SRTs vary in their skills, and there is nothing wrong with admiring an outstanding one. Climacus himself admires Socrates in this way. But in such admiration one must always keep in mind that there can well be others who are just as outstanding, and even if this present one is the most outstanding in the entire history of the human race, still he is only outstanding, not indispensable.

The utter contrast between Jesus and the SRT is obvious. The pupil of an SRT must, if he is properly to learn from him, in a certain sense forget him; but a disciple of Jesus, if he forgets him or treats him as in any way dispensable, forfeits the relationship by which he partakes of the salvation that Jesus offers. The SRT's entire educational project assumes that his pupil might have come to this understanding on his own and at most needs a lot of help; salvation by Jesus assumes that sin, from which the believer is to be saved, is a condition impossible for him to escape on his own. The disciple needs not just help, but something like a miracle by which he gets a new start.

To get his comparison off the ground, Climacus designates both Jesus and the SRT as "teacher," though for Jesus' primary role as savior this epithet is misleading. As Climacus remarks, "The one who not only gives the learner the truth but provides the condition is not a teacher" (14). It is not primarily by teaching that Jesus saves, but by dying. He saves by standing in the place for sinners. But what is the place for sinners? We use the word "stand" in an extended sense, because the place for sinners is not a place in which literally one stands; it is a place in which one hangs—and suffers and bleeds and dies. Climacus could, of course, just as well have got his comparison off the ground by designating the SRT and Jesus both as "savior," but if one had something like Christian salvation in mind, the epithet would again be misleading. The primary work of Jesus and the primary work of the SRT are indeed so different that one might wonder how it could occur to

Climacus to compare them. This is in a way just the impression that Climacus wants to convey, though of course, since the book is structured around just this "comparison," it conveys it only indirectly. The form of the book is entirely unstable: the reader who takes seriously the project of comparing Socrates and Jesus as teachers ends up staring at the abysmal disanalogy between the two.[9]

So how did Climacus come to compare the Socratic teacher and the Christian savior? Climacus looked about and saw that many people who claimed to be teaching Christianity were in fact teaching paganism. Climacus has enormous respect for paganism, especially as represented by Socrates, but less for something that at bottom is paganism yet parades about as Christianity. This is what happens when Christ is presented as one whose essential (that is, saving) role is to evoke in the "believer" a religious insight, or to stimulate him to a change of character. This is to present Christ not as the Lord of the universe whose death saves his disciples from something they could never save themselves from, and who demands that we cling to him for dear life, but instead to present him as one more religious teacher among many—even if he is the absolutely greatest and profoundest teacher and the best man who ever lived, so extraordinary in his power to evoke this insight and to alter people's character that he has the right uniquely to be named "redeemer." In a moment I shall have a brief look at three presentations of Christ that fall into the confused paganism against which Climacus's book is designed to inoculate us.

Before I do that I want to explain the word "grammatical" as I have used it a few times already and will continue to use it throughout this reading of *Fragments.* (My usage derives loosely from Ludwig Wittgenstein.)

The grammarian of English studies structural features of a language already in being. His task is therefore descriptive, and his success is measured by the general validity of his remarks about English as it is spoken and written by the people who speak it and write it best. But the grammarian's descriptions can be turned to a normative use. People who are not complete

---

[9]Since the role I have undertaken is unraveler of the irony rather than perpetrator of it, I shall often write "teacher" rather than teacher when the epithet refers to the god in time, as a gentle reminder of its impropriety. When Climacus speaks in the *Postscript* of "the contrast of the form" of the *Fragments* with its serious conceptual content, "form" can be read as having a double referent: the deductive form of the thought experiment and the form of a comparison between Socrates and Jesus. Even the "form" in the second sense is ultimately ironical, for a serious comparison presupposes some common category within which the comparison is carried out. But in the present case the category of teacher soon shows itself incapable of supporting this weight, and the upshot of the "comparison" is that no comparison is possible.

masters of English are taught the grammarian's principles, not because they have a rarified academic interest in the "structure" of their language, or because they ought to have an interest in such things, but because, being unsure about English, they can be helped by the discipline of reflection about the structure of their language to keep their English usage from failing at certain points. That is, they study grammar as a discipline for improving their practice of speech and writing. What most of Climacus's points in *Fragments* amount to, once they are disembedded from the irony, is something analogous to the grammarian's remarks about the grammar of a language. He is not inventing a religion or theology, or redoing Christianity, any more than a sober grammarian is inventing or redoing English; he is describing it, producing a perspicuous representation of certain basic features that are already there. Also like the grammarian's remarks, Climacus's representation of Christianity, if he can get it across, can correct and forestall errors in the practice of Christianity, errors that constitute forms of degeneration of Christian faith.[10]

In chapter one of *Fragments,* Climacus makes various observations in comparing the Christian savior with the Socratic religious teacher, which can be summarized in such remarks as, "The particular identity of Jesus Christ becomes indifferent if his role as savior is construed as the evoking of religious insights or the stimulation of religious character-traits." This remark is grammatical in that it captures a general feature of Christian thought and so can function as a rule for it—just as a grammarian's comment about the use of the partitive in French captures a general feature of that language. But the grammar of the French partitive is easily mastered. Millions of Frenchmen pass through life virtually untempted to violate the rule that the grammarian brings to formulation. By contrast, Climacus's point is deep—so deep that by its help we can see that some of the greatest theological thinkers of an age have been gibbering ungrammatical theology. Simple though it is when once we see it, it is a point that, for one reason or another, Christian thinkers are wont not to see. Our purblindness perhaps owes more to moral failings such as worldliness and want of courage than to weakness of intellect; and for this reason Climacus has felt compelled to present this simple thought in the context of an intellectual seduction. His remark stands guard at the

---

[10]I am indebted to Paul L. Holmer, in lectures and conversations, for the suggestion that many of the essential points in Climacus's writings are best construed as "grammatical remarks." For a rich discussion and extended application of the grammar metaphor to Christian theology, see his book *The Grammar of Faith* (San Francisco: Harper & Row, 1978), esp. ch. 2. The claim he makes there—that theology is grammar—is, however, different from the point that I have adopted from him about the status of Climacus's remarks. It further extends the grammar metaphor.

Christian thinker's door, bidding him daily to resist the temptation to see Christian salvation in Socratic terms, on pain of turning the "depth-grammar" of his discourse into paganism, however clothed its outer skin may be in the language of evangelical theology.

Perhaps I should now say something about the relationship between theology proper and what Climacus is doing, which might be called theological grammar. Statements like "subjectivity is truth," "a Socratic Christ is impossible," "God's existence cannot be proved," "no man has ever seen God," "the word of the cross is folly to those who are perishing," and many others can be fruitfully differentiated from theological remarks proper. Examples of the latter would be "God is love," "God was in Christ reconciling the world to himself," "The Lord is the everlasting God, the Creator of the ends of the earth," and so forth. For what Climacus's remarks do is to set the boundaries for the right use of theological remarks, to map their proper domain. For example, "subjectivity is truth" would be to say, "The remark 'God is love' (and many others like it) belongs (that is, has its truth) not in an idealistic system where it functions as a solution to some philosophical problem, but rather in the mouth and heart of an individual person (a subject) for whom it is the deepest happiness and profoundest caution of his life." Thus a Climackean grammatical remark is a remark about a (type of) theological remark, in which its relation to human life or to conceptual contexts other than Christian theology is clarified. It is not itself a theological remark—just as a remark of English grammar, though it be in English, is not a piece of primary English, but is rather *about* primary English—namely, how words are supposed to be arranged there. In the present sense of "grammatical," then, apart from some psychological points and the theological truth, which is the serious point of chapter two (that God so loved the world . . .), *Fragments* is a book of theological grammar.

The distinction between theology and theological grammar is not that between biblical statements and remarks about biblical statements. First, not all remarks about biblical statements are examples of theological grammar. Some are historical, philological, psychological, or even grammatical in the literal sense of being about the grammar of Hebrew or Greek. Second, some biblical statements are, in part, theological-grammatical remarks. For example, "the word of the cross is folly to those who are perishing" (1 Cor. 1:18) is a remark about such statements as "Christ died that you might have life," and what it says is that the correct use of this theological statement will involve a contravention of some of the thought patterns (the common sense) of people who do not heartily accept it. Consequently, one test of the theological correctness of a person's use of the statement about Christ's death would be to ask whether this use is such that anybody who understood the statement's import could accept it. If the statement is interpreted in such a way that anybody could accept it, then Paul's remark has the force of condemning that use of the statement as incorrect. The incorrectness need not always be grammatical (that is, having to do with the conceptual connections that the use of the statement trades on and evinces); it may be rhetorical (that is, may have to do with the clarity and psychological force of the presentation of the gospel of Christ's death). It is possible to get the conceptual connections right but to put them in such an obscure, abstract, or unforceful way that they are not understood. If statements about Christ's death are both grammatically correct and understood, Paul is saying, they will seem folly to those who are perishing.

* * * * *

EXCURSUS

I have said that Climacus's deduction of Christianity from the assumption of a non-Socratic "teacher" is an "indirect" way of getting across some incompatibilities. The two principal ones can be stated in the form of the following exclusive disjunctions:

(1) Either *the state of untruth out of which Jesus is thought to "save" is in principle corrigible by the effort of the "saved" individual* (call this proposition C), or *his particular identity is essential to his work as "savior"* (call this E), but not both.

(2) Either *the state of untruth out of which Jesus is thought to "save" is in principle corrigible by the effort of the "saved" individual* (C again), or *his activity as "savior" is not the occasioning of ethico-religious insights or character-traits* (call this ~ S), but not both.

Symbolizing these propositions, we get

(1) $(C \lor E) \cdot \sim (C \cdot E)$ and
(2) $(C \lor \sim S) \cdot \sim (C \cdot \sim S)$

But (1) is equivalent to the biconditional

(3) $C \equiv \sim E$

and (2) is equivalent to the biconditional

(4) $C \equiv S.$

(3), then, is equivalent to the conditionals

(5) $C \supset \sim E$ and
(6) $\sim E \supset C,$

and (4) is equivalent to the conditionals

(7) $C \supset S$ and
(8) $S \supset C.$

Translating back into English, we have

(5) If *the state of untruth out of which Jesus is thought to "save" is in principle corrigible by the effort of the "saved" individual,* then *his particular identity is not essential to his work as "savior."*

(6) If *Jesus' particular identity is not essential to his work as "savior,"* then the state of untruth out of which he is thought to "save" is in principle corrigible by the effort of the "saved" individual.

(7) *If the state of untruth out of which Jesus is thought to "save" is in principle corrigible by the effort of the "saved" individual,* then *his activity as "savior" is the occasioning of ethico-religious insights or character-traits.*

(8) If *Jesus' activity as "savior" is the occasioning of ethico-religious insights or character-traits,* then *the state of untruth out of which he is thought to "save" is in principle corrigible by the effort of the "saved" individual.*

Numbers five through eight are the backbone of Climacus's deduction. Considering the convertibility of exclusive either/or's into if-then statements, though of course it is nothing but logic, perhaps makes more intuitive how Climacus's efforts to impress (1) and (2) on his reader can take the form of a deduction.

* * * * *

SCHLEIERMACHER'S CHRIST

In choosing my examples of presentations of Christ that fall into the confused paganism against which Climacus would inoculate us, I shall neglect the rankest "liberals," who come right out and reject the New Testament's understanding of Jesus, claiming that he was in fact nothing but a religious teacher or some kind of existential paradigm. The writers I shall review would dissociate themselves from the simpleminded liberalism of Adolf von Harnack or the radical theology of Schubert Ogden. They would consider it essential to Christian theology to hold that Jesus Christ alone is the redeemer. What they have in common is thinking of redemption essentially as something that takes place in the consciousness of the "believer," or, as I have put it, as essentially an insight (most likely with ethical consequences) that the redeemer helps the "believer" to have. My examples are Friedrich Schleiermacher, Rudolf Bultmann, and John Cobb.

Schleiermacher wants to hold that Jesus occupies an absolutely unique place in religious history. His relation to his disciples is qualitatively different from Moses' or Mohammed's relations to theirs:

In Christianity the relation of the Founder to the members of the communion is quite different from what it is in the other religions. For those other founders are represented as having been, as it were, arbitrarily elevated from the mass of similar or not very different men, and as receiving just as much for themselves as for other people whatever they do receive in the way of divine doctrine and precept. Thus even an adherent of those faiths will hardly deny that God could just as well have given the law through another as through Moses, and the revelation could just as well have been given through another as through Mohammed. But Christ is distinguished from all others as Redeemer alone and for all, and is in no wise regarded as having been at any time in need of redemption Himself; and is therefore separated from the beginning from all other men, and endowed with redeeming power from His birth.[11]

What is it about Jesus that gives him this unique place?

Schleiermacher's view seems to be that Jesus is the only human being ever to have a perfect and perfectly constant feeling of absolute dependence. In the rest of us this "God-consciousness"[12] is more or less vague and fleeting, but in him it reached the ideal. Jesus is the redeemer in that, as the bearer of this ideal "God-consciousness" he has an extraordinary power to evoke in others an approximation to it:

> The original activity of the Redeemer is best conceived as a pervasive influence which is received by its object [i.e., the disciple] in virtue of the free movement with which he turns himself to its attraction, just as we ascribe an attractive power to everyone to whose educative intellectual influence we gladly submit ourselves.[13]

Indeed, so weak and fleeting is our feeling of absolute dependence apart from Christ's "influence" that Schleiermacher can say, "In truth He alone mediates all existence of God in the world [read: God consciousness or actual experience of absolute dependence] and all revelation of God through the world."[14]

> If it be the essence of redemption that the God-consciousness already present in human nature, though feeble and repressed, becomes stimulated and made dominant by the entrance of the living influence of Christ, the individual on whom this influence is exercised attains a religious personality not his before. Before this the God-consciousness was evinced only casually in isolated flashes, never kindling to a steady flame.[15]

So Schleiermacher maintains that the particular identity of Jesus is essential to the redemption of the disciple (translate: the moment has decisive significance). At the same time he maintains that Jesus' redeeming activity

---

[11]Friedrich Schleiermacher, *The Christian Faith,* 2 vols., ed. H. R. Mackintosh and J. S. Stewart (New York and Evanston: Harper & Row, 1963) §11, p. 57.

[12]For a presentation of Schleiermacher's notion of the feeling of absolute dependence, see my article, "The Feeling of Absolute Dependence," *The Journal of Religion* (July 1977). Here I put the expression "God-consciousness" in quotes because, as I argue in my article, it is incorrect to call the feeling of absolute dependence a consciousness of *God.* For Schleiermacher's own account, see nos. 4 and 32 of *The Christian Faith.*

[13]Ibid., no. 100.2, p. 427.

[14]Ibid., no. 94.2, p. 388.

[15]Ibid., no. 106.1, p. 476.

amounts to "influencing" or "stimulating" the disciple to a religious insight or religious personality change. If Climacus is right, Schleiermacher has undertaken an impossible task. He tries to combine concepts that belong to one sphere (the grammar of the Socratic teacher) with incompatible concepts from another sphere (the grammar of Christian redemption). In doing so, he has developed a religious paganism, only now a paganism with the detracting feature that it looks on the surface like Christianity. If Climacus is right, the use of Christian words like "redemption," "sin," and "Christ" cannot remedy the fact that the depth-grammar of these words makes them incompatible with Schleiermacher's essentially Socratic understanding of salvation.

We can see that Climacus is right if we press Schleiermacher with some hard questions: If Jesus' redeeming activity is accomplished by his stimulating the disciple to a personality change, why think that Jesus himself, the particular individual, remains essential to this work? Even if we assume that before Jesus came on the scene nobody ever had the feeling of absolute dependence, and that by his own experience of it he was the first to stimulate it, still it is hard to see why subsequent generations, who do not know Jesus "in the flesh," would not be able to receive this stimulation from others who had received the stimulation from others who had received it from others, and so forth, until we get back to the generation who received it directly from Jesus. In this case, though Jesus was the necessary point of departure for the tradition, there seems to be nothing about the nature of the redemption that would require subsequent individuals to hearken back to Jesus himself. If what makes the redeemer the redeemer is that he has the feeling of absolute dependence, then anybody who has the feeling is a potential redeemer, and if one generation forgot to communicate to the next that it was Jesus of Nazareth who had started the sequence, there seems to be no lessening of the redemptive power on this account. Indeed, it seems to be Schleiermacher's view that the redemptive power of Jesus (and not just the knowledge of it) is passed to subsequent generations by the community, the church, in which his power lives on. If this is so, then Jesus is only a first cause of a sequence of events that in no way depend for their future replication on remembering that it was he who started it all. Indeed, there seems no way to escape the conclusion that the "moment" can become a vanishing occasion, somewhat after the manner of the Socratic "moment."

Schleiermacher, however, refrains, for good Socratic reasons, from making the strong assumption we have just made about Jesus' historical significance. He does not believe that no one had the experience of absolute dependence before Jesus. The "God-consciousness" was "already present in human nature, though feeble and repressed." Or as Socrates might have put it, it needed "remembering" (See *Meno,* 8lb). Or as Climacus would say, the learner possesses the condition. Jesus is indeed only a stimulus to the development or clarification of something already present. He is, no doubt, according to Schleiermacher, an extraordinary stimulus in that he has the feeling of absolute dependence with unsurpassable clarity and constancy. This fact, if it were a fact about Jesus, would set him apart, somewhat, from other humans. But it does not set him apart as Jesus is set apart in Christianity—namely because he, and no one else among human beings, is God. In Schleiermacher's view, Jesus has in an ideal degree something that everybody has in some degree, and it is this that makes him "Redeemer." But in Christianity, Jesus has something that no one else has at all, namely Godhead. If Jesus is necessary at all in Schleiermacher's scheme, he is necessary only to the improvement of the feeling of absolute dependence, not to its establishment. When we see that "redemption" is really a matter of improvement rather than of anything that could appropriately be called a "new birth," it becomes even more difficult to see why a disciple, or even just some non-Christian who happened to have the feeling of absolute dependence a bit more strongly than average, could not stand in for Jesus as "Redeemer."

Climacus seeks to emphasize the point that in Christianity the particular identity of the redeemer is essentially linked with the nature of the redemption offered, and that anyone who understands redemption as a kind of stimulation to insight, moral improvement, or some sort of experience has so violated the grammar of the concept that a certain logical consequence ensues: the particular identity of the redeemer ceases to be essential. This is not to say, as Climacus seems to say by his program of deducing Christianity from the assumption of a teacher whose identity is essential, that it is inconceivable that there be any other system of beliefs than Christianity in which the notion of redemption makes the particular identity of the redeemer essential to it. It is to say, however (and this is Climacus's serious point), that any Socratic understanding of redemption, of which we have seen Schleiermacher's to be an instance, will entail that the particular identity of the redeemer is indifferent. An essential criterion for Christian theology is that his identity not be indifferent. Schleiermacher agrees to the criterion; this we can see by his fantasizing about Jesus' consciousness to preserve his uniqueness among humans.

Let us now consider another attempt, executed more than one hundred years after Schleiermacher and with all the advantages of the knowledge of his mistakes at its disposal. It too is an attempt to interpret Christian redemption along the grammatical lines of a Socratic relationship, while preserving the essentiality of the particular identity of the redeemer.

BULTMANN'S CHRIST

In an effort to escape liberalism and return to the Christianity of the reformation, Rudolf Bultmann emphasizes not the confrontation with Jesus himself, but with the "Word" of (or about?) Jesus. It is really the Word that saves, and it even turns out that the "Word" has two natures, just as Jesus was thought to have, according to the older Christology.[16] In an attempt to remain true to the New Testament, in which Christian preaching is distinguished from all other discourse by being a report about the atoning death and resurrection of Jesus of Nazareth, Bultmann holds that preaching's reference to the particular man Jesus is a *sine qua non* for its being Christian and for its being "saving." In an uncharacteristically strong statement that nevertheless indicates one side of his thought, Bultmann says, "The word of God is not some mysterious oracle, but a sober, factual account of a human life, of Jesus of Nazareth, possessing saving efficacy for man."[17]

What does Bultmann mean by "saving efficacy"? To be saved is, in Bultmann's thought, to be freed from one's past, to have one's self-understanding liberated in such a way that one faces the future, the dark unknown, with an utterly welcoming attitude. Our ordinary, inauthentic life is just the opposite of this. We cling anxiously to what is already established in our life—patterns of behavior and of thought, persons and possessions that give our life "meaning," skills and knowledge that we have accumulated and have at our disposal, and so forth. A person who lives in this way is violating his humanness, according to Bultmann. The hard core of being human is to be a decision maker, that is, to be confronted with options or openness. A person who lives inauthentically, in terms of what is set, established, given, already there, has to a great extent closed himself down, thus denying his own essence as an option holder. The result is anxiety and despair. From this self-understanding in terms of our past, our possessions, and so forth, we need to be freed into a total openness to possibility (the future).

Bultmann is obscure as to why the Christian kerygma alone can free people from their past. He studiously avoids Schleiermacher's kind of explanation, in terms of Jesus' unique consciousness and the extraordinary influence of his personality. It was Jesus' preaching, rather than his personality, that had this liberating effect on people. What is it about his preaching that renders it capable of bringing into the world something utterly new—human openness to the future? Jesus did not, according to Bultmann, claim

---

[16]For more on Bultmann's Christology, see Robert C. Roberts, *Rudolf Bultmann's Theology: A Critical Interpretation* (Grand Rapids: Wm. B. Eerdmans Publishing Company, 1976) ch. 3.

[17]Bultmann, *Kerygma and Myth* (New York: Harper & Row, 1961) 44.

for himself the power and authority of God, predict his own efficacious death, or perform physical miracles. He was an apocalyptic preacher who claimed nothing more than to be the authoritative "messenger of God bringing the final decisive word."[18] As such he and his preaching do not seem to be very different from any number of preachers who appeared before or after him. Yet for some unknown reason his preaching marks the absolute beginning of human authenticity. Before him, no human being had ever achieved radical openness to the future, and after him nobody achieves it except in confronting the particular preaching that he originated.

It is equally difficult to see why Jesus would have to be mentioned in subsequent preaching for it to have power to bring about openness to the future. After all, Jesus did not preach about himself. Bultmann goes round and round trying to explain how it happened that in the primitive church the proclaimer became the proclaimed—how the one whose preaching had "saving efficacy" became the subject of other people's preaching. If Jesus discovered a kind of preaching that had this extraordinary power, the reasonable course would seem to be to try to duplicate it as nearly as possible. So the apostles seem entirely wrong to start preaching differently—namely, to start preaching about Jesus. Yet Bultmann does not accuse the apostles of making a tactical mistake. It was, he says, the bare fact *that* Jesus preached that justified them in preaching about him in turn. This explanation commits Bultmann to just the contrary of his thesis that the Jesus kerygma alone frees people from their past. For if the fact *that* Jesus preached was sufficient to justify the apostles in calling him the redeemer of the world, it turns out that one is equally justified in calling Billy Graham and Harry Emerson Fosdick lords and saviors of the world.

Bultmann seems a little less vulnerable than Schleiermacher to Climacus's grammatical points about the dispensability of any Socratic teacher. Schleiermacher holds, in good Socratic fashion, that we all already have the feeling of absolute dependence in a weak and fleeting way, and what we need is the stimulation or influence of a great religious personality. Bultmann does not come out boldly Socratic, holding that we are all basically authentic. Instead, he claims that we are in bondage to inauthenticity, so that one and only one story—"a sober, factual account of a human life, of Jesus of Nazareth"—can set us free. Radical freedom from one's past is a state of mind that can be occasioned only by a confrontation with this particular story.

What grounds can there be for holding that a certain state of mind can be occasioned only by the hearing of a particular story? I submit that there are only two—the logical and the magical—both of which Bultmann will re-

---

[18]Bultmann, *Faith and Understanding* (New York: Harper & Row, 1969) 238.

ject. There is a logical connection between a state of mind and a particular story if we stipulate that the state of mind is that of believing the particular story. Obviously, if the state of mind called "redemption" is the state of mind of believing the story of Jesus of Nazareth, then a person cannot (logically cannot) be "redeemed" without having this particular story communicated to him, and if he believes it, then he is *ipso facto* (logically) "redeemed." But redemption is not, for either Bultmann or orthodox Christian theology, the state of mind of believing the story of Jesus of Nazareth. For Bultmann it is the state of mind of freedom from one's past, and the notion seems to be that somehow the belief in the story of Jesus causes this other state of mind. For orthodox Christian theology, redemption is not a state of mind at all, unless it be a state of God's mind; it is the state of being approved by God, despite one's sins, because of the merits of Christ. Faith is a state of mind that involves believing the story of Jesus, but believing the story is not faith and faith is not redemption; faith is the way the believer comes into possession of the redemption that was accomplished long before he ever had a mind.

If freedom from one's past is not identical with believing the story of Jesus of Nazareth, then how can it be that this and only this story can bring about this state of mind? The only remaining answer, it seems, is some version of magic. The claim would have to be that it is simply an inexplicable empirical fact that this story, and no other, has this effect on people. Bultmann sometimes suggests that Jesus' dying on the cross was crucial to the disciples' experience of freedom from their past. This makes some sense. If a man has the extraordinary power to attract disciples that the New Testament pictures Jesus as having, it is likely that the disciples' entire world view is going to be shaped by their relation to him. In addition, perhaps they have hopes that he will become a great political leader in whose government they will take part. When such a one is snatched from them and killed like a common criminal, it is likely that their state of mind will be one in which their entire "world" momentarily loses its meaning. Since he was everything to them, his death constitutes a kind of "death" for the disciples. If his influence is deep enough, and they do not quickly return to the former "meanings" of their lives, they may have a sense of being cut loose from their moorings in this world, radically freed from everything established, given, traditional, already there.

This construal of "redemption" would be a perfectly good way to avoid making the connection magical between Jesus or (possibly) the kerygma, on the one hand, and the disciples' experience, on the other. But if we understand the connection in this way—and it makes considerable psychological sense—it becomes impossible to hold any longer that Jesus alone can evoke radical openness to the future. The reasons Jesus evokes this state of mind are that (1) the effect of Jesus' personality on his disciples is that the deepest meaning of their lives gets intertwined with him; and (2) he is killed, preferably in absurd circumstances. But there seems to be no reason to doubt that the deaths of any number of "charismatic" leaders throughout history have had more or less this effect on their disciples.

Unlike Schleiermacher, Bultmann seriously attempts to avoid making Jesus a Socratic religious teacher so that he can claim that "the moment has decisive significance." He no doubt read the works of Climacus and learned this much: If the moment is to have decisive significance, then Jesus must not be conceived as merely stimulating the disciple to a "remembrance" of something that he already has access to. So he denies that human beings have a natural access to authenticity. But the denial cannot be sustained without resorting either to a violation of Bultmann's notion of authenticity, or to a magical view of the efficacy of the kerygma. If we retain the thesis that redemption is a state of mind of freedom from one's past, while rejecting the thesis that this state of mind is caused magically by the recital of a particular story, we must conclude that any number of stories, or better, confrontation with any number of individuals, may bring about the state of mind. Authenticity, as Bultmann conceives it, is the sort of thing to which human beings have a general natural access. It has the character of a Socratic "truth." The result, as Climacus predicts, is that the particular identity of the one who stimulates it is indifferent. Bultmann's theology, like Schleiermacher's, is not a variant of Christianity, but a thought system with an entirely different logic. This is not because they do not try to adhere to the criterion that "the moment has decisive significance," but because, given their notions of redemption, they cannot adhere to it. The depth-grammar of their thought will not allow it.

A "PROCESS" CHRIST

The third case by which I propose to test Climacus's exclusive disjunctions is the christological thought of John B. Cobb, one of the leading theological practitioners of "process philosophy."

In his essay "A Whiteheadian Christology"[19] Cobb seeks, with Alfred North Whitehead's help, to find a modern way of conceptualizing Jesus' identity and relation to God such that Jesus' identity will be "unique." At the same time he sketches Jesus' relationship to other human beings, what we might call his "saving efficacy." He seeks "a style of thinking [about Jesus] potentially more meaningful to us than the traditional formulations and yet in greater continuity with the tradition than modern radicalism."[20] Cobb is an

---

[19]In Delwin Brown, Ralph James, and Gene Reeves, eds., *Process Philosophy and Christian Thought* (Indianapolis and New York: The Bobbs-Merrill Company, 1971).

[20]Ibid., 383.

interesting test case because for him Jesus' role as "savior" is clearly Socratic; so if he can consistently hold onto the traditional notion that Jesus'
particular identity is essential to his role as savior, his "christology" will be
a counterexample to Climacus's either/or.

In his book *Christ in a Pluralistic Age*[21] Cobb expounds in more detail his
concept of salvation and of Jesus' saving efficacy. Salvation, for Cobb, is an
attitude or disposition to be "creatively transformed." "Expectancy, openness to the future, and freedom from the past are marks of the newly appropriate, primal response to God."[22] God (him)self is the creative
transformation of the world, the growingness-in-good-directions of it. This
growingness is also identified with human love (agape and empathy): "Not
only is the Logos [that is, God] itself love but the creative transformation
which is its work in us is human love."[23] Creative transformation is not a
radical break with the past, but precisely an openness to grow.

Jesus' saving efficacy is his power to effect creative transformation in
people. According to Cobb, Jesus does this primarily in two ways, by his
words and by his "field of force." In speaking about a coming kingdom, which
in many ways turns the present order upside down and yet at the same time
is a transformation of the present world, Jesus was able to occasion creative
transformation in some of his hearers. In the Sermon on the Mount, Jesus
creatively transforms the Jewish law; in the parable of the publican and the
Pharisee he creatively transforms the Jewish concept of righteousness; in
the parable of the workers in the vineyard he creatively transforms the Jewish concept of God's grace. In response to such words Jesus' hearers might
be offended, hardening themselves in their established patterns; or they
might respond with openness in creative transformation. The same can be
so for us, says Cobb: "The encounter with Jesus' words even today is an experience of creative transformation, or, otherwise stated, ... Jesus' words
can be the occasion for the deepening of the incarnation or the fuller realization of Christ."[24] The other way that Jesus saves is by setting up a "field
of force" into which persons can be drawn and in which they are creatively
transformed.

> The real past event of the crucifixion and resurrection of Jesus, involving his
> total being, has objectively established a sphere of effectiveness or a field of
> force into which people can enter. To enter the field is to have the efficacy of

---

[21]John B. Cobb, *A Whiteheadian Christology* (Philadelphia: The Westminster Press,
1975).

[22]Ibid., 89.

[23]Ibid., 85.

[24]Ibid., 99.

the salvation event become causally determinative of increasing aspects of one's total life. Faith, the ethical life, the church, and the sacraments are all to be understood in this context.[25]

The events of Jesus' life have become a factor in the history of which we partake, and these events have their ongoing effects in the present. Those who explicitly turn their attention to Jesus' person through meditation on him, through sacramental celebration, through Bible study and the preaching about him, as well as in other ways, open themselves especially to his creative transformation of them. Such attention is in aid of historical influence.

It seems plausible that not just any person saying the words Jesus said or being crucified and raised from the dead would therefore have the power that Cobb ascribes to Jesus, to effect creative transformation. There is something peculiar about Jesus' personal identity that gives him this power, and Cobb speculates about what that peculiarity is.

The human "I," as distinct from animal consciousness, identifies present experiences as in continuity with, or better, as arising out of and incorporating, past experiences. (A rabbit's or sheep's "I," if one wishes to name it thus, is just one experience after another without this objectifying sense of unity.) Thus, one can see that the human "I" in its most basic manifestation already has the form of creative transformation. The personal "I" in the strict sense comes into existence only when the subject begins to take an instrumental attitude towards his emotion and reason, not identifying himself with these functions, nor indeed with any of the physically and culturally determined experiences he has, but critically taking responsibility for such experiences and their outcomes. Of this "I" Cobb says, "Such a structure gained effective entry into the human scene first in Israel and is most clearly represented by Jeremiah."[26] The prophet is forced to this ethical transcendence of his given self by the absolute call of the divine "I," which calls into question the Jewish status quo and further calls Jeremiah publicly to call it into question on His behalf. Thus, the call of God to the prophet is a call to creative transformation of himself and his nation and one that raises the prophet's "I" to a qualitatively higher constitution, of which creative transformation is the explicitly accepted, objectively luring norm. This call of the Logos is in tension with other dispositions in the prophet—private interests and projects, comforts, friendships, established patterns of thought and life, the tendency to self-protection, and so forth.

The "I" of Jesus, as Cobb speculates about it, is best understood in contrast with this prophetic "I." Jesus' identity, like Jeremiah's, is constituted

---

[25]Ibid., 117.

[26]Cobb, *Process Philosophy and Christian Thought,* 391.

by an extraordinarily vivid consciousness of "the lure of creative novelty that is the immanent Logos."[27] In Jesus, unlike Jeremiah, nothing in his appropriation of his past stands in tension with his consciousness of the call to creative transformation.

> In the structure now under consideration, the "I" in each moment is constituted as much in the subjective reception of the lure to self-actualization that is the call and presence of the Logos as it is in continuity with the personal past. This structure of existence [is] the incarnation of the Logos in the fullest meaningful sense.[28]

Jesus' unperturbed unity of will with the principle of creative novelty is what constitutes his unique "I" and explains his authoritative demeanor and his independence of appeal to tradition or even to God as an external authority.

> He spoke on his own authority which was at the same time the authority of God. The "I" of Jesus, rather than standing over against the divine "I," identified its authority with that of God. Among the religious leaders of mankind this is a unique role.[29]

Our question on behalf of Johannes Climacus is: Does this constitution of Jesus' identity make him essential to "salvation" conceived as creative transformation? Or, is there anything about this "salvation" that makes it impossible that it be effected by some other teacher, or indeed by no teacher at all?

Cobb is clear that the principle of creative novelty is not itself uniquely present in Jesus; it is, according to him, only the extent and the way that it is present that is unique. Even Jesus was, according to Cobb, probably "not continuously free from the tension between his "I" and the Logos."[30] Strictly speaking, Jesus was only sometimes the incarnation of God. At other times, like that of the temptations in the wilderness, the struggle in Gethsemane, and so forth, his structure of existence was more like that of Jeremiah.

So the picture of "untruth" or sin implied by Cobb's soteriology is Socratic: It would be melodrama and utterly inaccurate for Cobb to speak of our being dead in our trespasses and sins. Asleep, yes, and in need of a Jesus or a Jeremiah (or a Socrates) to wake us, but certainly not dead, not in need of rebirth. Jesus saves by "reminding" us of the potential for creative transformation, a condition that is already present in each of us.

Since for Cobb, Jesus is not identical with God, but is only a human being who is from time to time perfectly tuned into the principle of creative nov-

---

[27]Cobb, *Christ in a Pluralistic Age,* 139.

[28]Ibid., 140.

[29]Cobb, *Process Philosophy,* 392.

[30]Cobb, *Christ in a Pluralistic Age,* 142.

elty (that is, the Logos), there is no reason why others could not have a strictly analogous personal identity. Of course it may be, as Cobb speculates, that there have been, in fact, no other human beings who were as utterly open to the Logos as Jesus was. If so, this is just an accident of history. As Cobb says, "There might be someone of whom history has left no record who was constituted much as Jesus was, but that is idle speculation. So far as we know, Jesus is unique."[31]

Even if Jesus is unique as in Cobb's construction, it would be extremely implausible to claim, and Cobb does not claim, that Jesus is the only savior. Perhaps he is, in all of history, the most powerful begetter of creative transformation. But one can think of hundreds of figures in history who have, to one degree or another, opened their fellows to creative transformation. A successful defense of the claim that Jesus is "unique," even uniquely related to God, and yet a Socratic "savior," would not be enough to confound Climacus. What is needed is a defense of the claim that Jesus is uniquely able to save and yet a Socratic "savior." Cobb's Christology is not even an attempt to defend *this* claim.

THOUGHT IN THE THERAPEUTIC MODE

I think I hear someone say: "Your interpretation of Climacus's first chapter has a ring of truth about it, and it is certainly startling, to say the least, how he has penetrated (both analytically and prophetically) to a simple archetypal and theologically fundamental mistake that invalidates whole tomes and systems of supposedly Christian thought authored by some of the most learned doctors of the modern church. But what a frivolous person Climacus is, indeed. For if you are right, he has buried this simple but far-reaching thought—that a Socratic Christ is impossible—in an elaborate joke. If he is, as you claim, a lover of the truth, why doesn't he present his discovery in a direct, unencumbered, and honest statement, with the elegant simplicity that befits it?"

The answer has to do with Climacus's book not being an effort at doctrinizing, in the manner of most philosophy and theology, but of communicating. Its purpose is not just theoretical, but therapeutic. The truths that are the serious content of the book could indeed be stated straightforwardly and with elegant simplicity, and I tried to do just this back in the introduction. However, Climacus's book is designed not just to present these ideas, but to inculcate them—and to inculcate them in people who are armed with a peculiar set of defenses against them. It is for sophisticated people, in fact for people whose very sophistication keeps them from reckoning with these simple truths. Climacus's first chapter is designed to seduce "Hegelians" into

---

[31]Ibid.

a conceptual inoculation against the kind of mistake that Schleiermacher and Bultmann make. Let me now spend the rest of the present section explaining the pivotal terms of this proposition: "seduce," "conceptual inoculation," and "Hegelians."

Hegel starts with the idea of "pure Being" and deduces, over many hundreds of pages and through tortuous processes of thought, not just Christianity but also Absolute Spirit, of which Christianity is a somewhat primitive, inadequate, and one-sided form, thus completing a rational system showing the necessary interconnections of everything that is. Climacus starts out, not with pure Being, but certainly with next to nothing, and gets Christianity—a more modest achievement, befitting an author of philosophical fragments. Like Socrates, who by his humble demeanor seduces sophists into recognizing the paltriness and incoherence of their ideas, Climacus coyly beckons "Hegelians" to join him in something that for them is surely very easy and elementary—a little "thought experiment." As it dawns on the reader that the deduction, which for him is the heart of the matter, is a joke, two things happen. First, the inaudible laughter to which he begins to feel his intellectual style and commitments subjected, encourages him to objectivize them; the unreflective seriousness with which he habitually treats them is, at least for the moment, divested of its virginal immediacy.

Then something else happens (ideally). Since he is not told just what is wrong with the deduction, he will nervously begin to look it over again, to examine it more closely for flaws. The more he subsequently works critically through the details, the more he will have had impressed upon him the facts of grammar that are Climacus's serious point. The disjunction between the Socratic teacher and the god in time, which on the surface of the exposition is subservient to the deduction project, is really what Climacus wants to communicate to his reader. The disjunction, with its attendant grammatical points, is in a way too simple for a sophisticated reader to worry over. If the disjunction were presented in direct discourse, the reader would be likely to acknowledge it hurriedly and then go on—perhaps to develop a Christology similar to Schleiermacher's or Bultmann's. A psychotherapist does not seek merely, like a lecturer on diagnostics, to make this or that point about the etiology of a patient's condition; he wants the point to sink into the patient's consciousness so that it can have consequences for his behavior and self-understanding. Similarly, Climacus does not want merely to make the distinction between the SRT and the Christian savior, or even merely to convince someone of it, but to impress it upon his reader. Or better, he wants to seduce his reader into impressing it upon himself.

Since the reader has such a strong tendency to "forget" this simple truth—since he so easily falls back into the more natural understanding of Jesus—Climacus does not write the truth straight out, but embeds it in a puzzle that will occupy the reader intensely for a time, during which he will be insensibly drilled in the disjunction. To this end it is artful that the "dialectical knot" be fairly complicated and fairly tightly tied. For otherwise the process of untying, which constitutes the therapy, is over too soon and the inoculation may not "take." If it does take, however, the "Hegelian" reader will never again be the same in his thinking about Jesus Christ. Of course, he does not necessarily become an orthodox believer hereby, but if he is not a believer, he will have become clear about it in a way that certain kinds of theologians are systematically inclined not to be.

Socrates' irony consisted in approaching one or another self-styled wise man with an air of humility and a declaration of ignorance, and then beginning to question him, "in order to learn from him." What arose out of the questioning was not the knowledge that Socrates purported to be seeking, but the revelation that the wise man did not know what he thought he knew. Of course, Socrates could have gone about town proclaiming, unironically, that the sophists did not know what they were talking about. The proposition would have been no less true if merely asserted baldly. But it would certainly not have had the same educative effect on sophists and those under their spell. Even if Socrates had gone about town with a list of refutations of the sophists' propositions, neatly detailed and conclusively argued, it would not have had the effect that his irony had. For the easy response of the wise men might have been, "Well, this is another theory. We have our own." Of course, there are always ways of patching up one's case, or at least making it look patched up. Irony is a tool for use on complacent holders of entrenched positions, positions that have become so much a part of the intellectual landscape that direct refutations do not pry their adherents loose from them. In Kierkegaard's day, as in ours, there are circles in which adherence to a Socratic understanding of Jesus is so unreflective that no direct refutation of it, from Scripture or by direct conceptual analysis, is likely to affect the adherents. In this circumstance, an ironic discussion is in order.

We are clear now about "seduce' and "conceptual inoculation." But who, precisely, is the "Hegelian" reader? Since Hegel's philosophy and something like his version of Christianity reigned among the intelligentsia of Climacus's day, there is little doubt that he is addressing people who are more or less directly influenced by the Prussian philosopher—certified Hegelians. But it would be a mistake to think that Climacus's therapy is narrowly tailored to the doctrines or assumptions or personality disorders peculiar to readers of the *Phenomenology* and the *Encyclopedia.* We have already seen what appropriate targets Schleiermacher and Bultmann and Cobb are, diverse though they are from one another and from Hegel. None of them, for example, has any stake in the thesis that reality is so constituted that beginning with the idea of pure being, we can deduce by necessary steps a system of thought that encompasses all reality. Nor do they share Hegel's other basic assumption, that concepts evolve other concepts out of themselves by generating their opposites and then mediating the "contradiction" thereby produced. One does not have to be literally a Hegelian, or ever to have heard of Hegel, to be captivated by Climacus's thought experiment. Being captivated by it—that is, taken in long enough by the irony to be motivated to untangle the dialectical knot—is the only prerequisite to entering upon the process of inoculation. On the other hand, if being "Hegelian" means being the sort of Christian who stands in need of inoculation—in need, that is, of being viscerally clear about the impossibility of a Socratic Christ—then we are all "Hegelians." For the tendency to domesticate Jesus in this way seems to be woven into the fabric of the human mind.

CHAPTER 2

THE GOD
AS TEACHER AND SAVIOR
(A POETICAL VENTURE)

CLIMBING HIGHER
(A LOVE STORY)

CHAPTER TWO OF *PHILOSOPHICAL FRAGMENTS* is outwardly a continuation of the project of thought undertaken in chapter one—that is, the effort to see what follows from the assumption of a "teacher" whose presence and particular identity are necessary conditions of his "teaching." In particular, this chapter advances to the inference that such a teacher must be the god incarnate in the form of a human, suffering servant. There is in chapter one the derivation that the teacher must be the god, and of course a general indication that he does his teaching in time, but no indication that the god must be in the form of a man, much less that this man must "be forsaken in death, absolutely the equal of the lowliest of human beings," his entire life being a story of suffering (32).

Despite the continuity, there is an important difference in the style of thought employed here, to which the reader is alerted by the subtitle of the chapter: "(a poetical venture)." Chapter one was a bit like a lecture in a priori dogmatics—rather schematic and didactic. Chapter two, by contrast, is a love story—economically told and liberally sprinkled with inferences and conceptual remarks, yet full of pathos. The main part of the reflection achieved in it—that is, the deduction—takes the form of solving a problem that is posed for a very peculiarly situated lover, namely the god: How shall the god come into a freely reciprocal love relationship with a human being? The answer is that the only way he can do so is to become "the humblest" of all human beings.

The problem, as Climacus expounds it, turns on the concept of equality. Between the Socratic teacher and his pupil there exists a natural equality. He has learned through others, and others learn through him. He owes to others precisely as much as he is owed by others—namely, in a certain sense, nothing whatsoever. Furthermore, the process of discussion by which his pupils learn from him is one in which he often learns a thing or two, and their questions often educate him as much as his do them. Socrates' "rare loyalty" (24) was the perfect consistency with which he humbly expressed this equality with his pupils, always refusing the posture of superiority that other teachers are wont, so unthinkingly, to adopt.

If the teacher is the god, there is no such equality: the pupil owes everything to the god, while the god owes nothing to the pupil. According to Climacus, this fact immediately raises the subsidiary problem of what can possibly motivate the god to come into a teaching relationship with the pupil. His answer is that since the god is the unmoved mover, he cannot be moved by any need for something outside him, but must move himself. Moreover, to Climacus this implies that he must be motivated by love, "for love does not have the satisfaction of need outside itself but within" (24). If it must be the god's love that moves him to act, then what he desires to establish by his act must be a love relationship with his pupil; for "just as his love is the basis, so also must love be the goal, for it would indeed be a contradiction for the god to have a basis of movement and a goal that do not correspond" (25). Thus it follows from the assumption that the teacher is the god, that the goal he has in mind in assuming the role of teacher is to establish a love relationship with the pupil.

If there is no equality between the teacher and the pupil, how is such a love relationship, which presupposes a mutuality of affection and understanding, ever to be realized? Indeed, says Climacus, this love (which is initially entirely on the side of the god, since the pupil has no understanding of it) "is basically unhappy, for they are very unequal" (25). The god's unhappiness is different from the unhappy love often found in the world, which derives from the lovers' inability to realize their union. Here the barrier is more radical: for without the necessary mutual understanding, there is no love relationship at all. Accordingly, the problem that generates the movement of thought in chapter two is this: How can the god, who is so vastly superior to the potential disciple, establish a love relationship with him? This problem, says Climacus, is one that only the god could have, and "no human situation can provide a valid analogy, even though we shall suggest one here in order to awaken the mind to an understanding of the divine" (26).

Climacus's chosen analog is a king who falls in love with a humble maiden. How shall he be united with her in love? The question is not, How shall he be united with her in marriage? For a king, that is an easy question. He wants a real love relationship with her, and that involves a meeting of the minds between them, an equal bearing of confidence on the part of each. There is a chasm between the kingly mind and bearing and that of the humble maiden, however, and the king is faced with an anguishing problem. As Climacus notes, the analogy breaks down at a number of points; but it does vivify the lyric of this "poetical venture."

The problem that the god faces, then, in "unfathomable sorrow," (28) is this: The one whom the god loves is unable to understand him because of this chasm of "inequality" that yawns out between them. "The learner is in untruth, indeed, is there through his own fault"[1] (28). He could turn his back on the learner, and be within his rights; but he loves the learner, and so refuses to do this. Yet he must be very careful of any expedient he may devise for establishing the love relationship. The king, if he is not careful, may dazzle the maiden and cause her to cower in fear or worship him in mindless admiration, rather than look him firmly in the eye with the regard of confident, womanly love. All the more must the god take care as he approaches the learner from across the abyss of their inequality; for the approach, taken in love, runs the very real risk of offending the learner, driving him still deeper into his guilt, and alienating him still further from the one who loves him.

There are only two kinds of way the requisite equality could be achieved: The god could elevate the learner to equality with himself, or he could humble himself to equality with the learner. Climacus deduces the latter from the unsatisfactoriness of the former.

There are two possible forms of elevation: First, the god might change the learner into some form that would allow him to take great pleasure in the god "and let the learner forget the misunderstanding in his tumult of joy" (29)—the misunderstanding being the fact that the learner is in untruth by reason of his own guilt. This would be a deception of the learner and thus inconsistent with a genuine love relationship, which presupposes frankness and mutual transparency. The other possibility is that the god can show a side of himself to the learner that the learner will find very attractive, "making [the learner] forget himself," (29) and giving him the false impression of

---

[1]Niels Thulstrup comments with multidimensional impropriety, in a note on Kierkegaard's relation to St. Anselm and Hegel, that "Kierkegaard . . . maintains that the necessity of the Christ-revelation cannot be drawn from the fact of sin." (in his Commentary, printed with *Philosophical Fragments,* trans. David Swenson and rev. Howard Hong, Princeton University Press, 1962) 199. First, Kierkegaard does not hold that the necessity of the Christ-revelation can be drawn from anything whatsoever. Unlike Anselm and Hegel, he is not in the business of a priori Christology. Johannes Climacus seems, to a very superficial reading, to be in this business, but indicates clearly at the end of his chapters that he is not. This suggests that the deduction of the "Christ-revelation" contained in the chapters is a piece of irony. Third, within the ironical deduction, as Climacus presents it, the fact of sin is essential. The entire argument of chapter two turns on the notion that between the god and the pupil there is a chasm of inequality. This "inequality," as it turns out, amounts to the fact that the god is holy and the pupil is in untruth by reason of his own guilt (see 28f.).

being in a love relationship with the god. (Presumably the god would not show himself to the learner as holy, as righteous judge, since this would cast the learner into despair; perhaps he would show himself in some spectacular and fascinating way as the creator of heaven and earth and their beauties.) This method too presupposes a lack of candor on the part of the god, and a deception of the learner—both about his own nature (namely his guilt), and the nature of the god (namely his holiness)—and this is incompatible with perfect love.

Since an elevation of the learner fails to bring about the love relationship, it will have to be accomplished by a humbling of the god. At this point Climacus introduces yet another assumption, namely that the learner must be not a selected human being, but any one whatsoever. "Let the learner be *X*" (31). (He gives a rhetorical justification of the assumption: "For if even Socrates did not keep company solely with brilliant minds, how then could the god make distinctions!" [ibid.].) But since *"X"* includes the lowliest human being, it follows that the god must take the form of the lowliest. "But the lowliest of all is one who must serve others—consequently, the god will appear in the form of a *servant*" (31). Since all deceit is ruled out by the concept of love, the god cannot be merely dressed up, as it were, like a human servant; he must actually become such. This in turn implies that he will actually suffer all things—actually, because he has in truth *become* the lowliest man; suffer, because he has become the *lowliest* man, and suffering is the lot of such a man. Added to this suffering is the incalculable suffering of misunderstood godly love; for by no other expedient will his love of the learner have any chance of fruition, and yet this expedient is fraught with dangers and frustrations for the love relationship.

This, then, is the argument of chapter two:

(1) The teacher-learner relationship assumes an "equality" between the two.

(2) Such equality exists naturally between the Socratic teacher and his pupils, but necessarily not between the god and his; so in the latter case the equality must be established by an *act*.

(3) But nothing could motivate such an act on the part of the god except love, and what love desires is necessarily a love relationship; so what the god is aiming at in performing this equalizing act is to establish a love relationship between himself and the learner.

(4) There are only two ways the equalizing can be done, by elevating the learner or by abasing the god; but elevation of the learner entails deceit, which is incongruent with love. So the equality must be accomplished by the abasement of the god.

(5) The learner must be *X*, which includes the lowliest; so the equalizing entails that the god becomes the lowliest of all human beings. And this in turn entails that he becomes a suffering servant.

Thus, starting with the observation that a teacher-learner relationship involves equality between the two, and applying this insight to the case in which the moment has decisive significance, we have deduced that the teacher (namely, the god) must be incarnate as a suffering human servant.

Climacus ends chapter two, as he did chapter one, with an imagined conversation between himself and an accuser: "What you are composing is the shabbiest plagiarism ever to appear" (35). The conversation takes the form of a playful inquiry, by Climacus, into the question of who might be the author of the poem if he is not, and his conclusion is that neither any human individual nor the race at large is the author: "Forgive me my curious mistaken notion of having composed [the poem] myself. It was a mistaken notion, and the poem was so different from every human poem that it was no poem at all but *the wonder*" (36). The conversation and its conclusion create a dissonance with the reasoning that has preceded. The merry reader suddenly wonders what all this sensation of forward motion has really amounted to.

THE LOVE OF AN UNMOVED MOVER

Like chapter one, chapter two is rhetorically smooth and exhilarating (much more so than my rather boney rendition of it). Its "poetic" character perhaps discourages the reader still further from attending very closely to the joints in the argument. The reader is delighted by the sublimities to which he can climb on Climber John's ladder. If he slides back down, attentively feeling the rungs (as he is indirectly encouraged to do by the conversation between Climacus and his interlocutor at the end of the chapter), he will discover that hardly any of them will bear the weight of inference. It was by sleight-of-foot that Climacus gave the impression of achieving the sublimities. Let us turn to an examination of the rungs on this portion of Climacus's ladder.

First a word of caution is in order. The conceptual analysis that I shall give in this and the next section, while invited by the form of *Fragments* as a whole and even of chapter two in particular, nonetheless clashes with the poetic garb in which this stretch of Climacus's text is arrayed. My approach is doubly dubious because I believe that the serious point of the chapter is not a conceptual or grammatical one (as the serious point of chapter one was), but instead something that is best expressed poetically. I freely admit that I do not know how to examine rigorously the dialectic of this chapter while preserving the lyrical impression that is essential to it. Perhaps it is inevitable that, for the moment at least, I "practice lyricide because I became 'angry with the thought.' "[2] So I suggest proceeding to page 57 if one is offended at all the logic-chopping that is going to intervene.

First, without the principle that a teacher-learner relationship is always based on equality, we would never get the problem that the teacher-god can supposedly solve only by becoming a suffering servant. But why should we accept the principle?

The epistemology upon which Socrates based his humility was the doctrine of recollection. No one ever gives knowledge to anyone, according to the theory of recollection; therefore, regarding knowledge the teacher owes the pupil exactly what the pupil owes the teacher—namely, nothing whatsoever. Hence the equality of the teacher and pupil. It is a deceit, however, and part of the Socratic irony to infer that since no one owes his knowledge to anyone else, therefore teachers owe their pupils as much as pupils owe their teachers. For teachers do something, even on Socrates' account, and to be fair we must measure the pupil's debt in terms of what his teacher does, not in terms of something it is impossible to do. If one accepts the theory of recollection, then one must calculate debt not on knowledge imparted, but on remembrances occasioned. The doctrine does not deny that one person can be better than others at stimulating remembrances and can thus have others indebted to him as a teacher. Socrates was presumably himself a teacher without whom many of his pupils would never have come to the rich "remembrances" to which he stimulated them by his conversation. So even if one accepts the doctrine of recollection, it does not follow that teachers and pupils are all equal, if one means by equality equally indebted to one another with respect to the teaching.

But even if we granted that every human teacher is as indebted to his pupils as his pupils are to him, we would need a strong warrant for claiming an analogy, in this respect, with the god as teacher. One of the most important serious points of Climacus's book is that there are some fundamental differences between the relationship that the god in time sustains with his learner and that which the Socratic teacher sustains with his. Indeed, the differences turn out to be so fundamental and so enormous that—as I remarked in the section "JESUS AND SOCRATES"—the reader who begins to untie the ironical knot of the book comes to see that there is a fundamental impropriety in comparing Socrates and the god in time under the single rubric of "teacher." So the question the discerning reader will now want to ask is this: Even if I disregard that Socrates is being ironical when he asserts humbly that as teacher he is the perfect equal of the poorest of his students,

---

[2]See H. A. Nielsen, *Where the Passion Is: A Reading of Kierkegaard's Philosophical Fragments* (Tallahassee: University Presses of Florida, 1983) 31.

what right have I to assume that the god in time must share this feature with Socrates (since he shares so few others with him)? In Climacus's text, however, no warrant is offered for this hardy assumption. The question is not raised; the issue is ignored.

As the deduction develops Climacus seems to derive the necessity for equality between the god and his pupil from the fact that it is a love relationship that is to be established between them. Thus:

(1) There is no love relationship between persons who do not mutually understand one another, and

(2) There is no mutual understanding between persons who are not equals.

(3) Therefore there is no love relationship between persons who are not equals.

The trouble is in the second premise. It obviously seems correct that some mutual understanding must be present in any reciprocal love relationship: if a child is to reciprocate his parents' love, even minimally, he must have some understanding of his parents' motives, needs, and so forth. But it is certainly not true that the two parties must be equal in their understanding of each other. The love between a ten-year-old and his parents may be reciprocal, and in that sense a full love relationship, without his understanding of them being equal to theirs of him. He loves them in his way and according to his understanding, and they love him according to theirs. This kind of unequal love relationship would seem to be as good a model as we can find of the love that can exist between God and a human being. (The argument obviously works no better if we mean by "equal" not "equal in understanding," but "equally indebted to one another." For the ten-year-old is also more deeply indebted to his parents than they are to him.) So the argument is a failure which says that equality must be established between the god and his disciple if the relationship between them is ever to be one of reciprocal love.

But in talking about the love relationship we are getting ahead of ourselves. For in the context of the deduction it is a new result that the relationship between the learner and the teacher-god is one of reciprocal love, and we must examine how it was achieved. Climacus argues to this conclusion in two steps. The first establishes that the god, in seeking to initiate a relationship with the learner, can only be motivated by love. The second establishes that what he is seeking is a reciprocal love.

The first conclusion is achieved in this way: The god desires to come into a teacher-learner relationship with some human being. (This is part of the hypothesis of Climacus's thought-experiment.) But the god is an absolutely peculiar sort of agent in that he is the unmoved mover. That is, nothing outside of himself causes him to do anything. Or, to use Climacus's words, "There . . . is no need that moves him" (24). If he is not moved by some need, then the only remaining possibility is that he is moved by love, "for love does not have the satisfaction of need outside itself but within" (ibid.). Therefore, on the assumption that the god is moved to come into a teaching relationship with some human being, it follows that he must be motivated by love.

To say that the god is the unmoved mover evidently does not mean that he is not moved or that he has no desires. To admit that he is motivated at all seems to imply that he has desires. If we admit that he loves, we must admit that he desires, for even a love that did not desire reciprocation would at least desire the welfare of the beloved. Climacus, in accordance with the biblical tradition, depicts the god as deeply desirous of a relationship with the disciple. But if the god's being the unmoved mover does not mean that he has no desires, it must mean that his desires, unlike human desires, do not have their source outside of him. They are uncreated, and in this sense "eternal." Now, does it follow from the fact that the god has only uncreated desires that the only desire motivating him to come into a teaching relationship with some human being is love for that human being? We must be careful here not to let our biblically based concept of God influence our judgment; for Climacus is here engaged in a thought-experiment in which, at this point, it has not yet been established that the god is a god of love. Indeed, that is precisely what he is trying to establish with the present argument. It seems clear to me that if we do not presuppose that the god is a god of love, it does not in the least follow from the added assumption that his desires are all uncreated that his motive must be love. For all we know at this point, the god may be motivated by the uncreated desire for fun and may want to establish this relationship with the learner because it promises to be amusing.

Someone may object, in Climacus's defense, that my rebuttal of his argument has left out part of what he means by calling the god the "unmoved mover." He may mean by this epithet that the god's desires are uncreated, but he also stipulates that the god "is not moved by need." But to say that the god acts out of the desire for fun is precisely the sort of thing that is ruled out by denying that the god is moved by need. If, so the objection goes, you rule out all desires that in this sense are feelings of need, there is, as Climacus suggests, no other motive left than love.

To evaluate this objection, we must ask ourselves what is meant by "need" in the expression "is not moved by need." If the argument is to be coherent, whatever feature of a motive is designated by "need" must be present in all motives except love. If it is absent in any motive other than love, then from the fact that the god "is not moved by need," it would not follow that his motive must be love.

In the human context we often distinguish needs from motives such as the desire for fun. "Why does Mr. N work twelve hours a day?" "He does not need to; he just does it because he enjoys his work." Obviously this is not the contrast that Climacus has in mind. Two more alternatives are suggested by one of Climacus's sentences: "But if he moves himself, then there of course is no need that moves him, as if he himself could not endure silence but was compelled to burst into speech" (24). The last part of the sentence suggests that a "need" may be a compelling, irresistible desire, one that the subject of it feels he must fulfill. A desire that is not a "need" in this sense would then be a relatively mild desire, such that if the desire is not fulfilled, this fact will not occasion any great anxiety, frustration, or grief. This also cannot be what Climacus has in mind, for two reasons: First, the love that he attributes to the god is indeed a compelling desire and so, according to this interpretation, would have to be classified as a need. (When the god's desire to teach the disciple is frustrated, he experiences "unfathomable sorrow" [28].) Second, surely a person could have any number of mild desires that were not love: for example, a mild desire to hear some piano music, read a logic book, or drive a nail. Another possibility is suggested by the first part of the sentence quoted above: If the god moves himself, then he is not moved by need. This suggests that a need is a created desire. This is the interpretation I assumed in my first rebuttal of Climacus's argument, when I said that we have no grounds for ruling out other uncreated desires than love.

I can think of one other possibility. Perhaps Climacus has in mind Kant's distinction between being moved by inclination and being moved by duty. It would be in the spirit of Kant to equate being moved by inclination with being moved by need, and being moved by duty with moving oneself (freedom). By this interpretation the god's love would not be a desire at all, but a case of acting, apart from inclination, purely on considerations of practical reason. I doubt that Kant's theory of ethical motivation is psychologically coherent. But it seems obvious, from the passionate desire for fellowship with the "learner" that Climacus attributes to the god in chapter two, that this is not the contrast he has in mind with the expressions "moved by need" and "moved by love." To use Kant's term, the god is very much moved, as Climacus represents him, by inclination. I admit that if "moved by need" means for Climacus anything other than "moved by a created desire," I cannot think what it might be. (Note that in his discussion with his interlocutor at the end of the chapter, Climacus seems to interpret the "poem" as implying that the god does need the learner: "For if the god gave no indication, how could it occur to a man that the blessed god could need him?" [36])

The argument by which Climacus pretends to deduce that the god's motive in establishing a relationship with the learner is love seems to be a non sequitur. From this fact, if it is a fact, it does not follow that Climacus has made a mistake. For we have good reason to think that his real source for the claim that the god loves the learner is the New Testament, and that his argument here is in the style of Socrates, who used to say cunningly to one or another sophist, "There is something that has been puzzling me."

Once Climacus has derived the assertion that the god's motive in entering into relationship with the learner must be love, he goes on to argue that what the god wants in the relationship must be reciprocal love: "But just as his love is the basis, so also must love be the goal, for it would indeed be a contradiction for the god to have a basis of movement and a goal that do not correspond" (25). In other words, it would be inconsistent for a person who was motivated by love not to desire that the beloved love in return; and all the more would this be so for the god (presumably because of his eminent rationality). Here, it seems to me, we have an inference that follows. It would be inconsistent for a person both to love another and not to care whether the other loved. The reason is that loving a person is a very high state of personal well-being, and fully reciprocal love is an even higher state. Thus one who rationally loves another necessarily desires such states of well-being in his beloved.

CUR DEUS HOMO

We are now ready to examine the main dialectical transition in chapter two, by which it is concluded that if the god is to bring to fruition his love for the learner, he must become a human, suffering servant. For this purpose Climacus plays loosely with three conceptual polarities that seem to be for him roughly interchangeable. These notions are equality/inequality, mutual understanding/lack of mutual understanding, and guilt/righteousness. These are, of course, very different sets of notions, and consequently Climacus's loose interchanging of them in the derivation is exasperating to the analytic reader who wants to know just how the transition works.

As we saw, the chapter begins by setting up the problem in terms of inequality: Any teacher-learner relationship supposes equality between its members; but there is no such equality between the god and his potential disciple. Climacus must arrive at the conclusion that it is necessary for the god to become a man, and to this purpose the concept of equality seems admirably suited. As noted, it is difficult to get very far with the concept of equality all by itself, because there seems to be nothing intrinsically problematic in the notion of inequality between the members of either a love relationship or a teaching relationship.

Better suited to creating a problem for a love relationship is the lack of mutual understanding between its members, since some mutual understanding is a necessary condition of mutual love. The deficiency in this concept, for Climacus's purpose, is that if it is used all by itself, it does not seem to require a solution as radical as the god's becoming a man. Why not just a gradual rapprochement involving occasional meetings and increasingly heart-to-heart discussion?

The deficiency in both the concept of inequality and that of a lack of mutual understanding is that they do not set up the problem in the same terms as does Christian theology, namely that the barrier to fellowship between God and man is sin. Consequently, Climacus has to interpret the inequality between the god and the learner, as well as the lack of mutual understanding between them, as the learner's being in untruth (see 28). However, the difficulty is that the solution—that is, the god's becoming equal with the learner—seems to entail that the god must become not only a human being but a human being who is in untruth. This is bad divinity and must be avoided. Climacus's footwork on this transition is so sprightly and shifty that it is difficult to keep track of him.

At any rate there are, according to Climacus, only two ways this equality/ mutual understanding/overcoming of untruth can be achieved: By raising the learner to equality with the god, or by lowering the god to equality with the learner. Any attempt to deploy the first expedient, says Climacus, will involve deceit of the learner, and this is not congruent with love. Climacus discusses two possible forms of elevation of the learner.[3]

In the first form, "The god would . . . draw the learner up toward himself, exalt him, divert him with joy lasting a thousand years (for to him a thousand years are as one day), let the learner forget the misunderstanding in his tumult of joy" (29). This, says Climacus, would involve a deceit of the learner. The reason this has to be so is not immediately apparent. The picture is that the god miraculously transforms the learner in such a way that he becomes capable, in some heretofore impossible way, of joyfully experiencing the god. If the barrier to fellowship between the god and the learner was a lack of mutual understanding between them, the present expedient strikes one as a pretty good bet for solving the problem. Perhaps the learner is miraculously endowed with a new faculty by which he can now understand and appreciate the god. Why could this not be the basis of the new fellowship between them? If there had previously been a "misunderstanding" between them, why shouldn't this miracle of elevation dispel it?

---

[3]We might remark that his notion of equality is shifty right here. The result he has his eye on, up the dialectical ladder, is that the god must become a man. So one might suppose that his concept of equality will imply that if two things are "equal" at least they must belong to the same kind. From this it would follow that the elevation of the learner to equality with the god would have to involve the learner's becoming a god. But Climacus does not apply the concept of equality the same way in considering the two alternative methods of equalization. Indeed it is hard to see how the expression "equality with the god" is at all apt for the two forms of elevation that Climacus discusses.

The answer to our perplexity is that Climacus is not using the word "misunderstanding" in a standard way. What he refers to as misunderstanding here is really guilt. A misunderstanding, when it is cleared up, no longer exists; but a guilt, when a guilty party has mended his ways, does not go away, even if it is forgotten. The only way to get rid of guilt is to atone for it, or perhaps also to be forgiven, provided the forgiver is sufficiently authoritative. (Here we are, of course, not talking about guilt feelings, or guilt scars, but about guilt.) It is for this reason that giving the learner a new faculty and letting him forget the misunderstanding in tumultuous joy would not be a solution to the problem. The barrier to fellowship is guilt, and guilt cannot be done away with by this sort of method. When we see that the problem is guilt, however, it begins to look strange to propose overcoming it by some act of equalization of the guilty and offended parties. What is essential about guilt is not the inequality of the two parties, or even any misunderstanding between them. On the other hand, if we do not think of the problem as guilt, but merely as a lack of mutual understanding, it is difficult to see why this method of equalization would not be a perfectly fine solution to the god's problem.

The second elevative method is this: "The unity could be brought about by the god's appearing to the learner, accepting his adoration, and thereby making him forget himself" (29). Here, as in the former method of "equalization," the god reveals himself to the learner and thus brings about some kind of understanding between himself and the learner. The only difference, as far as I can see, is that this is now achieved without a miraculous transformation of the learner. The god just "shows himself." This method, like the other, fails only on the assumption that the barrier to fellowship is not just a misunderstanding or an inequality but guilt. If the problem is guilt, then neither equalization nor revelation would be the essential solution; instead, atonement would be necessary.

Climacus continues:

> If, then, the unity could not be brought about by an ascent, then it must be attempted by a descent. Let the learner be X, and this X must also include the lowliest. . . . In order for unity to be effected, the god must become like this one. He will appear, therefore, as the equal of the lowliest of persons. But the lowliest of all is one who must serve others—consequently the god will appear in the form of a servant. (31)

This solution, claims Climacus, must be the one that the god, in his love, will choose. Since the objection to the elevative methods was that they involved deceit, Climacus must claim that this method involves none. He emphasizes that this method does avoid deceit in that the god actually becomes a humble servant human being. Only the god can work such a miracle: "For this is the boundlessness of love, that in earnestness and truth and not in jest it wills to be the equal of the beloved, and it is the omnipotence of re-solving love to be capable of that of which neither the king nor Socrates was capable, which is why their assumed characters were still a kind of deceit" (32). The god, in his descending equalization with the learner, does not de-ceive him because, unlike the king who is dressed up as a peasant and unlike Socrates who disguises himself in his "ignorance," the god really is a hum-ble man.

Notice: The argument's appearance of success depends on equivocating about the word "deceive." The way the learner is deceived by the elevative methods is that his guilt remains unremoved, whereas the way he avoids being deceived in the descending method is that an appearance to him (namely the appearance of the god as a humble servant) is veridical. To prove that the descending method avoids the difficulty that vitiates the elevative methods, Climacus must show that by becoming a humble, suffering human servant, the god takes away the guilt of the learner—that he accomplishes something more than a revelation. There is nothing in the idea of descend-ing equalization (incarnation) that implies atonement for guilt, and Clima-cus does not claim that there is. He simply pretends that he has shown the descending method to be preferable to the elevative ones.

INSPIRATION AMIDST THE ARGUMENT

Climacus's argument is so full of holes that no careful reader will trust it as a vessel for its precious contents, and yet unless we perform some such analysis as I have just done, we are not likely to put our finger on the trou-bles. One has a frustrated awareness that the argument is not working, yet it never breaks down so obviously that the reader commits the volume to the flames. As long as we do not carefully (and laboriously, I might add) take the argument apart, it is captivating. So by making the fallacies explicit, I have given a false impression of the book. It probably looks worse to you now than it did before you read my analysis, and worse than it will look if you take the time to reread Climacus's chapter. "Worse indeed," you may retort, "but if the hatchet job you have just done is anywhere near correct, the impression is not false. It's a bad book, and that's all there is to say."

But there is more to say, and my discussion in the previous chapter did give a false impression of Climacus's second chapter. By focusing as I did upon the logical transitions, I almost entirely failed to give any impression of the poetic force of the chapter. We must remember that the chapter is not only a further climb up Climacus's ladder but also, importantly, a love story and an essay of the imagination, a poetical venture. The serious purpose of the chapter is different from the ostensible purpose of continuing the thought experiment, even though the two purposes are accomplished more or less simultaneously.

In section four I presented some theses that express (but hardly communicate) the serious intent of *Philosophical Fragments*. One of these had to do with the origin and character of the relationship between Jesus Christ and his disciples as a love relationship: "The relationship between Jesus Christ and his disciple is initiated by God's loving and sacrificial act of becoming a man." This, so bland when stated as a thesis and so boringly unoriginal when presented as a piece of theology, is nevertheless the main serious point of chapter two.

Whereas a number of the other serious points in *Fragments* are what I have called "grammatical"—points about peculiarities in the behavior of concepts within the Christian context—the present point might better be described as "personal." Accordingly, the way to communicate it (and let us not forget that *Fragments* is largely a piece of communication) is not to induce the reader to dwell upon certain broad differences between, for example, Socrates as teacher and Christ as "teacher" (chapter 1), or between the warrants required and adequate for most historical assertions and those appropriate to the assertion that Jesus of Nazareth is God (chapters 4 and 5), but instead to tell a story in a heartfelt manner. To make this thesis come across to the reader, Climacus will seek to make the reader privy—by poetic means and by an exercise of the imagination—to the inmost heart of God. The serious thrust of this chapter, insofar as it is different from chapter one, is not dialectical at all but poetic.

If chapter one, with its nonironical upshot, is an example of theological grammar, aimed at immunizing the mind against a type of heresy grounded in following up a false analogy between Christ and other "teachers," then chapter two (in its nonironical aspect), while tirelessly retaining its hold on the original grammatical strand, is an example of *preaching*. In other words, it is aimed at touching the reader's heart and cultivating in him, through the use of imagination, a passional appreciation of God's love for him in Jesus Christ. Just before he introduces the story of the king who loved a humble maiden, Climacus says that while there is really no valid human analogy to the problem that faces the god in his love for the learner, nevertheless he will suggest one "in order to waken the mind to an understanding of the divine" (26). The real point of chapter two is this quickening of the mind to an apprehension of the divine love.

If I have two friends, van der Kooy and van der Veen, and I want to quicken van der Kooy's mind to an apprehension of van der Veen's love, I will best do it by storytelling. What will be in my stories? Broadly, two kinds of things: accounts of some of van der Veen's deeds, which arise out of his love for van der Kooy, and accounts of some relevant states of van der Veen's mind (especially some of the patterns of van der Veen's griefs and joys). The most elegant way to get van der Veen's love across to van der Kooy, however, will be to pick some significant sacrificial act that van der Veen has performed on van der Kooy's behalf, and then to give, as it were, the psychohistory of that: to tell of van der Veen's deliberations, his hopes for his friend, his anxieties about whether van der Kooy will really be bettered by his act, the pain of sacrifice as he renounces benefits to himself to gain benefits for his friend. If after hearing the story van der Kooy remains unmoved, then we must conclude that he is "a lumpish soul with as much character as a small coin bearing the image neither of Caesar nor of God" (28).

This is what Climacus has done in chapter two. He has given us an imaginative essay upon the heart of God—a love story, the psychohistory, as it were, of the act in which God so loved the world that he gave his only Son. He suspends this touching story in the unsubstantial net of his hilarious deduction: the "problem," which generates and is generated by the artificial dialectic of the chapter, is also the crux of the story that reveals the heart of God. Then when the story has been unfolded, he turns around (in the conversation with the interlocutor at the end of the chapter) and with a breath of laughter dispels the illusion that it was the net that supported the love story. The story did not arise out of the deduction, nor is it hypothetical in the way that everything generated by the deduction would have to be: the story is in fact the miracle, a word from God himself.

The deductive links in chapter two are much weaker than those in chapter one. Shall we say that the poor arguments are part of Climacus's irony? Did he intend them as a trap for Hegelians? I do not know, and I think it does not matter. What we can say, if my analysis of the serious purpose of chapter two is correct, is that Climacus does not have much stake in the correctness of the arguments. Here the situation is different from that of chapter one. For in chapter one, the serious point was that there are some logical incompatibilities that theologians such as Bultmann and Schleiermacher violate to their theological and religious peril. Logical incompatibilities can be turned into two-way entailments, however; so the serious point Climacus is making permits him (and commits him to) a certain tightness in the deduction. The entailments of the deduction have to be on the whole correct if the incompatibilities, which are the serious point, are to be genuine. In the present chapter the serious point is not one of theological grammar but of theology. And indeed this point is one that needs to be impressed on the reader by something like preaching. Preaching can be correct both theologically and rhetorically even if the inferences that may appear in it are invalid (though the inferences can certainly be annoying and distracting to somebody who notices that they are invalid). So the poverty of the arguments in chapter two need not affect its serious point.

Chapters one and two together symbolize a dual fact about faith and reason: Chapter one tells us, indirectly, that faith has a definite logic, which to violate is to lose the faith. There are not only Christian truths that must be adhered to if the faith is to remain intact; there is also a certain logic or grammar to those truths, a certain matrix in which they belong and outside of which they lose their identity as Christian. But in addition to the grammar of faith, there is what we might call its rhetoric. Faith also has imaginative content; it is emotion. Faith, if it is to arise in a person's heart, requires inspiration, a kind of breathing in, an appeal to the heart. This is what chapter two does for us: It takes the faith whose logic has been so masterfully outlined in chapter one (and whose name has not yet been uttered, though every reader is assumed to know its identity) and touches the reader with it in the manner of excellent preaching.

CHAPTER 3

THE ABSOLUTE PARADOX
(A METAPHYSICAL CAPRICE)

THE PARADOXICAL PASSION
OF "THE UNDERSTANDING"

IN CHAPTER THREE Climacus undertakes to prove that the god in time, the suffering servant, was a folly to the Greeks and a stumbling block to the Jews. Or, to put the matter in Climacus's language, the god in time was the absolute paradox.

Climacus's main serious thesis in the beginning pages is that "understanding," or better, man as possessor of "understanding" in its various facets, is ambivalent about some things that are beyond his understanding: On the one hand, man as thinker has the presentiment that if he does not get beyond the limits of the "reasonable," he will never find himself, his health, his happiness, his salvation. On the other hand, also as thinker, he is disposed to be offended when it is proposed to him to live out his life in terms of something that cannot be justified by reference to the canons of understanding. The form in which Climacus expresses this thesis is, however, mostly unserious:

> For the paradox is the passion of thought, and the thinker without the paradox is like the lover without passion. . . . But the ultimate potentiation of every passion is always to will its own downfall, and so it is also the ultimate passion of the understanding [Forstand] to will the collision, although in one way or another the collision must become its downfall. (37)

I will explain in a moment why I think there is jest in this passage, but first we must get a little clearer on what "understanding" denotes, for it expresses a many-sided concept.

The aspect of the concept suggested in the first sentence of the quote is this: "Understanding" denotes the powers, dispositions, talents, and skills that enable the activity of reasoning—that is, arguing and explaining, giving reasons. If we say, "that woman's powers of understanding are extraordinary," we may mean that she is very good at arguing and explaining. Paradoxes are a strong stimulus to such activities: when we find ourselves wanting to say two things that seem inconsistent with each other, we busily set about to see which of the beliefs is false, or how they can be reconciled. Paradoxes in the strict sense are not the only stimulus to arguing and explaining; sometimes we are incited by burning questions that do not have the form of a paradox. Perhaps Climacus wants to extend "paradox" to cover all burning questions of a sort that we might hope to answer by reflection. He trades on the arguing/explaining aspect of "understanding" a few pages hence when he supports his contention that the god is unknowable to the understanding by showing that the teleological and ontological arguments for the existence of God do not work.

But the activities of "understanding" are governed by norms, explicit and inexplicit, and it is sometimes these norms that are referred to by the word "understanding." These norms will include the (mostly unspoken and perhaps unspeakable) rules for what counts as good evidence, and rules of inference such as "if 'p' is true and 'p implies q' is true, then 'q' is true." In many people's minds "understanding" will also encompass the incoherent rule, "never believe anything without sufficient evidence." These principles constitute part of what we might call common sense or being a reasonable person.

But something else we might call common sense—something else supplying normative rules that govern people's thinking in a broad sense—is the fund of notions by which the individual makes sense of his own life. These are primarily value-principles, and some examples might be, "Git whal the gittin's good," "Happiness is being respected by your community," "The most important thing in life is to avoid injury, sickness, and death as long as possible," "Financial security is essential," and so forth. These norms are also part of common sense, and a person like Socrates who flouts them is thought by the "reasonable" people to be a little wobbly in the head. Because Climacus is also trading on this aspect of "understanding," he can take Socrates—who though "a connoisseur of human nature," could not make up his mind how to conceive himself—as an illustration of the paradox of understanding's "willing its own downfall." In this context Socrates' willing the downfall of understanding would not mean his defiance of *modus ponens* or any such thing, but his skepticism about the common-sense categories of self-understanding.[1] It would be his yearning, as a thinker who was long

---

[1]Climacus speaks rather obscurely, and even paradoxically, about Socrates and self-knowledge in these opening pages. When he says, "Let us assume that we know what man is" (47), he is referring to Socrates' doctrine of recollection. To the question "What is man?" the doctrine answers (with lofty formality), "Each individual man is his own measure, in that each must take full responsibility for his self-understanding and his conduct; but also each man is the measure of mankind, for one man's eternal responsibility does not differ from another's." But Climacus also mentions

preoccupied with questions about what fulfillment for his own life might consist of, for something better than this common sense. Socrates' skepticism is in a way fulfilled in Jesus Christ, for to live and die as Christ did is to fill the void of Socrates' skepticism with a positive new conception of life, one that is necessarily polemical against "understanding" in the present sense.

Having said a few words about the "content" of the first few pages of chapter three, let us examine the "form"—that is, the argument leading to the conception of the absolute paradox. For though the conclusion is not drawn in these pages, there is a complete argument for the thesis that the understanding desires the absolute paradox as its (paradoxically) highest fulfillment. It goes like this:

> (1) The highest potentiation of every passion is always to will its downfall.
>
> (2) But the understanding's passion is generated by paradoxes.
>
> (3) So the highest potentiation of the understanding's passion must be the desire to encounter an absolute paradox, something that thought cannot think.

The argument as Climacus presents it is perhaps guilty of equivocation, since what generates a passion is not always identical with the object of the passion. In the paradigm case of erotic love perhaps the beloved is both the object and the generator of the passion. But though it seems true that paradoxes at least help generate the enthusiasm of reasoners, it is not so clear that what reasoners want to encounter is therefore paradoxes. One might plausibly think that while they are spurred on by paradoxes, what reasoners want to encounter is some consistent body of beliefs. The argument could perhaps be cured of this difficulty (and also generally improved) by removing the second premise altogether. Maybe it follows directly from the first premise that the highest passion of the reasoner is to find something that he cannot think through. That would seem to be a fairly good formula for the downfall of the passion of reason.

---

twice that Socrates, who above all people has come to grips with this doctrine of man, "is no longer certain whether he is a more strangely composite animal than Typhon" (48-49). Not only are these thoughts consistent; the second, interpreted as I am interpreting Climacus to be interpreting Socrates, is a natural consequence of the first. In the latter citation Socrates is speaking ironically: He means to castigate, indirectly, those who accept their self-understanding from their (temporal) social environment, not to express doubts about the doctrine of recollection. For that doctrine says (in Climacus's interpretation, anyway) that each individual must work out his own self-understanding by relating himself to what is eternal in himself. Therefore, people who adopt the common-sense values of their social environment are in violation of this doctrine.

   Our most pressing doubt, however, is about the first premise. Doesn't it
seem much more likely that the highest pitch of every passion is always to
will its own fulfillment? The serious import of this sentence is that the highest pitch of passionate thinking about how to live one's life results in a skepticism about the norms of self-understanding proposed by common sense.
But formally Climacus is here presenting it as a general principle from which
to deduce something about the absolute paradox, and as such it is outrageous. Instantiating the principle a few times, we get "The highest potentiation of the desire for wealth is the desire for poverty," "The highest
potentiation of the desire for fame is the desire for obscurity," "The highest
potentiation of gourmandism is the desire to taste something really revolt-
ing," and so forth.
   Comically, Climacus does hint at two extremely weak justifications of this
principle that so cries out for strong backing. First,

> It is the same with the paradox of erotic love. A person lives undisturbed in
> himself, and then awakens the paradox of self-love as love for another . . . the
> lover is changed by this paradox of love so that he almost does not recognize
> himself any more. (39)

The case would seem to go this way: A selfish young man wants pleasures
for himself. In the same mood he wants a lover too. Then he finds one, but
as his love for her deepens he becomes willing to give up his pleasures for
her sake. He loves her more than he loves the pleasures he derives from loving her. So, for example, if it is to her benefit that she not be his, but perhaps
enter a convent or become the lover of someone else, he might be willing,
out of love for her, to forsake his pleasures. Thus the initial desire for pleasure (namely self-love) has resulted in its downfall, the willingness to give
up pleasure.
   But this case does not fit the principle of which Climacus suggests it is
an illustration. For the principle says that the highest pitch of every passion
is to desire its own frustration (and only from this interpretation of the principle can Climacus derive that the understanding must desire to encounter
the unthinkable). But the lover does not *desire* to give up the pleasure of his
beloved's company, even if he is *willing,* for her sake, to do so.
   Climacus also seems to appeal, in support of his principle, to the case of
Socrates, who as a passionate inquirer after self-knowledge "no longer is sure
whether he perhaps is a more curiously complex animal than Typhon or
whether he has in his being a gentler and diviner part" (39). This too is not
an instance of the principle that the highest potentiation of every passion is
to will its own downfall. For even if Socrates did fail in his lifelong quest for
self-knowledge, there is nothing here to indicate that it had been Socrates'
will (conscious or otherwise) so to fail.

BELIEF IN GOD AND THE POWER
OF "THE UNDERSTANDING"

The next move in Climacus's larger argument is to identify the object of the paradoxical passion of understanding as none other than the god. Whether he accomplishes this identification by argument or by stipulation is not entirely clear. He certainly appears to try to prove that the god is unknowable to the understanding; for he spends a solid six pages ruminating about efforts to demonstrate the existence of the god by purely rational means, and the conclusion of his cogitations is that the thing cannot be done. So one might think that he has an argument, and it goes like this:

> (1) Whatever it is that the understanding desires paradoxically to know (and thus not to know since it hereby wills its own downfall) must be unknowable to understanding (for otherwise its passion might be frustrated by success).
>
> (2) But the god is unknowable to the understanding, because reasoning to the conclusion that the god exists always fails.
>
> (3) Therefore the god is what the understanding desires paradoxically to know.

If this is Climacus's argument, it commits the fallacy of affirming the consequent. It is like arguing that

> (1) Whatever is furry is warm.
>
> (2) Woodstoves are warm.
>
> (3) Therefore woodstoves are furry.

But maybe this is not his argument, for he seems at one point simply to stipulate that the god is what the understanding desires paradoxically to know: "Therefore, let us call this unknown *the god.* It is only a name we give to it" (39). If there is no argument, then of course there is no fallacy; but then we are given no reason for identifying the bearer of this name as the creator (if such exists) of nature, as Climacus does in the next few pages. For "the god" "is only a name we give to" the unknown. If it really were nothing but a name, then other names—for example, "the Loch Ness Monster" or "Little Stikefrick"—would do just as well. Climacus, however, would probably balk at such substitutions. If he called the unknown "Little Stikefrick" his train of thought would suffer arrested development. Furthermore, the first sentence following his long discussion of the impossibility of demonstrating the god's existence reads thus: "The paradoxical passion of the understanding is, then, continually colliding with this unknown" (44). I conclude, then, that Climacus's destructive discussion of traditional efforts to demonstrate the god's existence is part of his hilarious deduction of the absolute paradox; it is offered in support of the second premise of the argument outlined above.

I think this discussion also has a nonironical purpose. Climacus seriously believes that the existence of the god cannot be demonstrated, and this fact is related to the offensiveness we sometimes feel in the belief in God. This, of course, does not mean that no sound argument can be contrived whose conclusion is that God exists. Thus, in the spirit of George Mavrodes,

(1) If God does not exist, then neither do chipmunks;
(2) There are chipmunks;
(3) Therefore God exists

is a valid argument whose premises are true. Any number of such arguments can be devised, and Climacus does not deny it. He denies instead that any argument has the power to coerce a person, on pain of irrationality, to believe in God. I think he also means to deny the weaker thesis that there is some argument that makes it, on balance, somewhat more reasonable to believe in God than to disbelieve.

This he expresses by claiming that the existence of the god always emerges from the argument by a leap. This seems to be the original context for Climacus's use of the word "leap." That is, with respect to premises acceptable to any sane and intelligent person, plus the ordinary laws of reasoning, one can get to the belief in God only by jumping free of the premises or laws (that is, committing a fallacy). So far, then, leaping to faith is argument-relative. The person who believes in God without deriving his belief from premises would not, on this account of the leap of faith, gain his faith by a leap.

Climacus extends the sense of "leap" so that genuine faith—not just assent to certain propositions—is always a leap.[2] It is as though obviously true premises and unexceptionable rules of logic come to symbolize for Climacus the entire world of "common-sense" values—comforts, financial security, long life, health, respectability, and so forth. But from this world in which all of us are so inclined to find the meaning of our lives, Christianity, like Socrates, calls us away. In this extended sense, then, faith in God and Christ is always by a leap; it always calls for a break with common sense and so always appears to common sense as "paradoxical" (also now in an extended sense). As Climacus remarks in the *Postscript,* "The truth as paradox in the Socratic sense becomes analogous to the paradox *sensu eminentiori,* the passion of inwardness in existing becomes an analogue to faith *sensu eminentiori*" (185n). Climacus also believes that there is "something eternal" in the human self, a hunger for something different from the objects val-

---

[2]For an extended discussion of "the leap," in which Climacus trades on both the logical and the extended senses of the word, see *Postscript,* 90-97.

ued by this common sense, and that this something is intimately connected with the nature of the human self as a thinking or imagining being.

With these observations I think we can make positive sense of Climacus's saying that the desire to discover "something that thought itself cannot think . . . is fundamentally present everywhere in thought" (37). In *Fragments,* much of the discussion of "the understanding" would lead us to think that Climacus is talking about thinking in the sense of technical argumentation. However, he makes clear in the *Postscript* that "I speak merely of thinking as it is in the subjective thinker." And he says, "In seeking to transcend itself lyrically, thought wills the discovery of the paradoxical. This presentiment of thought is a synthesis of jest and earnest, and here all the Christian categories are to be found. . . . The last thing that human thinking can will to do, is to will to transcend itself in the paradoxical" (95). It is not the thinker as a *technical* thinker, attempting to prove the existence of God by the teleological or ontological argument, who wills to abandon himself to values contrary to common sense ("to transcend [himself] in the paradoxical"). It is rather the thinker who is seeking to make sense of his life, and to whom this "presentiment of thought" suggests that common sense is, for this purpose, bankrupt. Thus in the "leap" in the extended sense the thinker (and here we are all thinkers) makes the only sense that is ultimately sense for a human life, and this is different from making a mistake in an argument.

For a person who has been trained to think according to high standards of evidence and logic, the proposal to believe in God may appear offensive: The proposition "God exists" does not seem to be self-evidently true, but neither does it follow convincingly from any obviously true premises. So judged by the standards of "understanding" in this sense, the belief appears disreputable. This characteristic of belief in God would not offend compulsive reasoners if this belief were one that could be easily ignored. But the same people who feel the belief to be disreputable often feel it to be momentous. God is not a topic that human beings can discuss disinterestedly, all their posturing to the contrary notwithstanding.[3] So when the personal

---

[3] In a footnote that did not make it to the final draft of *Fragments,* Climacus expresses the belief that everyone, deep in his heart, knows that God exists: "But just as no one has ever proved [the God's existence], so has there never been an atheist, even though there certainly have been many who have been unwilling to let what they knew (that the God [*Guden*] exists) get control of their minds." *Søren Kierkegaard's Journals and Papers,* vol. 3, ed. and trans. Howard Hong and Edna Hong (Bloomington: Indiana University Press, 1975) #3606. John Calvin makes the same point: "Indeed, the perversity of the impious, who though they struggle furiously are unable to extricate themselves from the fear of God, is abundant testimony that this conviction, namely that *there is some God,* is naturally inborn in all, and is fixed deep within, as it were in the very marrow." *Institutes of the Christian Religion,* trans. Ford Lewis Battles (Philadelphia: Westminster Press, 1960) 1:3:3.

importance of belief in God is combined with the emotional demand in which we are nurtured from an early age by the agents of "understanding," then unless a person believes, he is offended.

The cure for offense is of course just to "relax," giving up the demand for "good reasons" in order to believe. Intellectuals who are also believers sometimes feel an ambivalence about belief in God: As believers they are happy, but as intellectuals they feel a gnawing discomfort, dissatisfaction, or embarrassment about their belief (unless they can convince themselves somehow that they do have respectable argumentative grounds for believing in God—in which case they are all the more vulnerable to embarrassment if they notice that these grounds are spurious). For them, as for the unbeliever, the cure for offense is to believe—in their case, to enter more deeply, more emotionally, more venturesomely, into the life of faith in God. Short of that, and perhaps in its aid, is to come decisively to grips with this fact about the logic of belief in God: that the belief cannot be founded on an argument. For if the believer can get a perspicuous representation of that state of affairs, then a healthy resignation will overtake the side of him that is inclined to demand valid inferences from true premises in all the connections of his life, and he will be freed from this compulsion—freed for a more serene God-relationship. In these pages on demonstrations of God's existence, clumsy though Climacus's effort sometimes is, this liberating, perspicuous view of the logic of belief in God is, I think, what he is trying to give his reader. Let us turn now to analyzing these pages.

A COUPLE OF WILD THRUSTS
AT NATURAL THEOLOGY

Before Climacus enters into his analysis of the particular efforts to demonstrate God's existence (the teleological argument and the ontological argument), he makes a couple of broadsides against the enterprise in general.

He begins by saying, "It hardly occurs to the understanding to want to demonstrate that this unknown (the god) exists" (39). He cannot mean this literally, since the idea has repeatedly suggested itself, and if it had not, there would be no need of his writing the present section. He must mean that although the idea has suggested itself to the understanding, this has been a fundamental mistake. Here is his reasoning: "If . . . the god does not exist, then of course it is impossible to demonstrate it. But if he does exist, then it is foolishness to want to demonstrate it" (39). Let us examine these propositions one at a time.

It is true that if God does not exist it will be impossible to prove that he does; for the conclusion of the proof will have to be "God exists," and if he does not this proposition is false and the argument cannot be sound, much less a proof. But this is no reason to think it a mistake to *try* to prove God's existence. Maybe the Loch Ness Monster does not exist; but that fact does not make it folly to attempt to prove that it does. Of course it would be non-sense for someone who knows that the Monster does not exist to undertake a proof that it does. But Climacus does not believe that anybody knows that God does not exist. So it seems that the first conditional does not support Climacus's claim that it is a mistake to try to prove God's existence.

The second says that if God exists, it would be folly to try to prove that he does. But why? A proof that God exists might be useful in two ways. First, it might be a way of finding out whether he exists. Even if there never was an atheist there is some sense in which people are in the dark about God's existence. It is surely not in general folly to try to discover the existence of things that exist. A successful proof might be enlightening; a failure would leave one in the dark, but none the worse for having tried. Second, even if the prover starts out knowing that God exists, either by the proof or in some other way, it may be useful to perform the proof to convince others, or because performing it will deepen the prover's insights into the conceptual connections involved and perhaps increase his confidence in the conclusion. Here we meet an oddity that runs through Climacus's discussion of proofs. He supposes that the only purpose a proof could have is that of generating the prover's conviction of the truth of the conclusion. If God exists, he thinks, it would be folly to try to prove it, "since I, in the very moment the demonstration commences, would presuppose it not as doubtful—which a presupposition cannot be, inasmuch as it is a presupposition—but as decided" (39). He seems to be saying that if I am convinced of God's existence when I begin the proof, then there is no point in doing the proof. But does it not very often happen in science and mathematics that a person starts out convinced of the truth of a proposition and then seeks, for various reasons, to find a proof of it?

A related argument is found on pages 43-44.

> If, at the moment he is supposed to begin the demonstration, it is not totally undecided whether the god exists or not, then, of course, he does not demonstrate it, and if that is the situation in the beginning, then he never does make a beginning—partly for fear that he will not succeed because the god may not exist, and partly because he has nothing with which to begin.

What does Climacus mean by "undecided"? Does he mean that the god's existence is not asserted in the premises, or that the prover is not convinced of the god's existence? Obviously the argument will not constitute a proof of the god's existence if his existence is asserted in the premise set. Climacus goes on to say that if the god's existence is "undecided," then the prover "never does make a beginning—partly for fear that he will not succeed because the god may not exist." But now the sense of "undecided" cannot be that the god's existence is not asserted in the premise set. For that fact would surely not cause fear of failure on the part of the prover. Here Climacus must mean by "undecided" that the prover is not fully convinced of the god's existence. If this is what is meant by "undecided," then it does not follow that if the god's existence is not undecided at the outset of the proof, then the proof is bound to fail. If a successful proof can be offered, surely a believer can offer it.

Climacus's second broadside against the enterprise of natural theology is to argue that it is impossible to demonstrate the existence of God because it is impossible to demonstrate the existence of *anything.* Existence "can never be demonstrated." The reason is that whenever one sets out to prove the existence of something,

> The whole process of demonstration continually becomes something entirely different, becomes an expanded concluding development of what I conclude from having presupposed that the object of investigation exists. Therefore, whether I am moving in the world of sensate palpability or in the world of thought, I never reason in conclusion to existence, but I reason in conclusion from existence. (40)

Is it true that we can never argue to a conclusion of the form "x exists," but always only to conclusions of the form "x (which we have *assumed* to exist) has characteristics A, B, and so forth"? The reasoning by which Urbain Leverrier discovered the planet Neptune would seem to be a counterexample to Climacus's principle. Leverrier deduced, from the anomalous motions of Uranus, that there must be another heavenly body in approximately such-and-such an orbit. Thus the existence of a hitherto unknown planet in our solar system was discovered.[4] There are a multitude of examples of reasoning in this pattern. I conclude that neither of Climacus's broadsides against the enterprise of proving God's existence works. Let us now take a look at his criticisms of two particular attempts to demonstrate God's existence.

THE TELEOLOGICAL ARGUMENT

The teleological argument attempts to demonstrate the existence of God by reference to nature. It says,

> Look at nature, with the beautiful and intricate interaction of its various parts, the evident fittingness of each element to its place in the whole. It is as impossible to hold that nature came into being without God as designer, as it would be to hold that a watch, found in a deserted place, had come into being without the help of human ingenuity.

---

[4]See Stephen Toulmin and June Goodfield, *The Fabric of the Heavens* (New York: Harper & Brothers, 1961) 254.

Climacus observes that anyone who finds this argument convincing does so because he conceives nature in the first place as God's creation. If he does not start with this assumption (or better, this way of viewing things), then he cannot get from an observation of nature's characteristics to the conclusion that the God of Hebrew and Christian faith exists.

The reason the inference fails is that nature is either noncommittal on most of the features that the Hebrew-Christian God must have, or, as Climacus emphasizes, has features that seem to be positively polemical against Christian belief. Perhaps the order in nature is evidence of some kind of designing agency, but this evidence is compatible with that agency's possessing a number of other features that would mean, for Christians and Jews, that the designing agency was not God. For example, to name three possibilities compatible with the designer hypothesis, perhaps nature "was only the first rude essay of some infant deity who afterwards abandoned it, ashamed of his lame performance; [or] it is the work only of some dependent, inferior deity, and is the object of derision to his superiors; [or] it is the production of old age and dotage in some superannuated deity, and ever since his death has run on at adventures."[5] Christians and Jews believe that God is *one,* and would refuse the name "God" to a task-force of designing and creating beings who managed to get up the present universe. What is there in nature from which we could conclude the impossibility or even the improbability of such a hypothesis? Again Hume's Philo:

> Were one deity antecedently proved ... who were possessed of every attribute requisite to the production of the universe, it would be needless, I own, (though not absurd) to suppose any other deity existent. But while it is still a question whether all these attributes are united in one subject or dispersed among several independent beings, by what phenomena in nature can we pretend to decide the controversy?[6]

Or perhaps the designer and constructor of nature is not the maker of the *material* from which he has constructed it (which we might suppose to be co-eternal with him). Whether a Christian would be willing to call such a being God would probably depend on the Christian's theological persnicketiness and on what other attributes we supposed this being to have.

One of the most important of these other attributes is moral goodness. But on moral issues nature seems entirely ambiguous: No doubt, she evinces some of what could be viewed as wisdom and goodness. Side by side with this she also evinces what looks to human eyes like wastefulness, cru-

---

[5]David Hume, *Dialogues Concerning Natural Religion,* ed. Henry D. Aiken (New York: Hafner Publishing Company, 1951) 41.

[6]Ibid., 40.

elty, arbitrariness, and indifference to human (and animal) concerns. If we try to base our belief in God on observation of nature, "Do we not encounter the most terrible spiritual trials here, and is it ever possible to be finished with all these trials?" (42) If one already believes in God, then one can see his hand in nature, for it is his creation. Then one either has, or supposes that there exists (though not necessarily available to us), a way of reconciling with this belief those features of nature that seem contrary to it. If someone thinks he believes in God because nature speaks of God, then he is miserably confused. Belief in God is rather a venture that defies certain observations of nature, much in the way a scientist may for the sake of his theory defy anomalous data and persevere. The difference between the believer, if he is mature, and the scientist is probably that the believer is resigned to finding no theoretical resolution, in this life, of the dissonance between what he believes and what he sees. But one of the principles of "understanding" current among us exhorts us to believe only those propositions that are borne out by, or are at least consonant with, what we can observe—or at the very least propositions that we can hope (sometime in this temporal life) to reconcile with what we see. So from "understanding" as this pattern of thought (and who among us does not at least feel a tug from it?) belief in God can appear offensive.

Climacus leads into his discussion of the teleological argument rather oddly by remarking that it is impossible to prove the existence of a particular human individual (for example, Napoleon) from his deeds, since if one describes the deeds without reference to their doer (and otherwise one is cheating), one cannot tell enough about the individual from the deeds to determine who he is. One can see from Napoleon's deeds that they had to be done by a great general, and so forth, but one can never infer validly that they must be the deeds of this particular man. The reason is that any number of people might have had the qualifications to do the deeds. But it does not follow from this that the god's existence cannot be proved from *his* deeds, admits Climacus, because the relationship between the god and his deeds is significantly different from that between Napoleon and his. "Between the god and his works there is an absolute relation. God is not a name but a concept" (41).

The point here is that the word "God" does not function as a proper name in this sense: A proper name does not essentially involve any description of its bearer, whereas "God" does. "God" means (among other things) "the one who made nature." To put it another way, the word "God" (like other concept-words, for example, "table," "number," and so forth) has implications, whereas proper names do not. The sentence "anybody who is God has to have made nature" is necessarily true, whereas sentences like "anybody who is Robert has to have . . . " are necessarily false since naming someone Robert has no implications for who he is, what he has done, and so forth. Admittedly there are descriptive names such as "Richard the Lionhearted," the "Left Bank," and so forth. But insofar as these names imply something about their bearers, they are not just names, but descriptions. Insofar as "Richard the Lion-Hearted" is just a name, it will be just as good a name if he becomes chicken-hearted. A thing or person gets his name by having it stuck on him, as it were. God, if he exists, gets his name by virtue of its fitting his identity. Names, strictly so-called, do not fit the identity of anything. Only descriptions and concepts do.

There is obviously another sense in which "God" is a proper name, and I do not think Climacus is denying this. We address God with "God," just as we address Robert with "Robert," whereas we do not usually, in polite company at any rate, address people with descriptions of them. Also, by virtue of God's being a concept-word, it is more proper to God (namely perfectly proper) than proper names usually are to their bearers. There may be thousands of people named Robert, but there is necessarily no more than one named God. There would be nothing in principle untoward about naming the oak tree in the backyard Robert; but it would be outrageous to name it God. To say that "God" is proper to God is of course not to put any restriction on the number of words that can possibly be used for God—"Dieu," "Elohim," "Gott," and so forth—but only to say that whatever word is used for God will function as a concept-word, whose concept implies that the one named by the word is uniquely named by it and, among other things, that he is the one who made nature.

So unlike Napoleon, who just happens to be the one who did what he did, God does not *happen* to have created nature; if he exists, then he is the only one who could have done it. One might be tempted to think that certain other consequences follow from the fact that it is implied by the concept of God that he created nature. One might think it follows that if anyone did it, God had to be the one. But Climacus is right in his criticism of the teleological argument: Even if we grant that nature's character makes probable the existence of some creator-designer, there remain creationist alternatives to the belief in God. The fact that God, if he exists, would have to be the one who created nature, does not help at all to rule out those alternatives; for it says nothing about whether he exists. Or one might even think, finally, that the concept of God itself somehow implies that he exists. This is the thesis of some forms of the ontological argument, and at the point in Climacus's discussion where this question comes up, he attaches a footnote in which his purpose seems to be perfunctorily to dismiss the ontological argument, as part of his general effort to show that "understanding" cannot provide the ground for belief in God.

THE ONTOLOGICAL ARGUMENT

The ontological argument comes in a number of versions, and Climacus chooses as his example a version propounded by Spinoza. Why he chose this version is unclear. If we were unkind, we might suggest that he picked it because it is such a pushover, and he was anxious to get on with other business. I am inclined to another hypothesis, having to do with the location of his volume of Spinoza on the bookshelf: I suspect that it was within arm's reach of Climacus's writing chair, whereas fetching Anselm would have required him to rise upon his legs. Perhaps this is why Climacus can say, speaking of *Fragments,* "such a book I do not need a long time to write."[7] By his own admission, you will remember, Climacus is a loafer from love of ease. But let us forsake these vain historical speculations and return to the metaphysical solidities of Climacus's caprice.

Spinoza's argument goes essentially like this:

(1) The more perfect something is, the more reality (that is, existence) it has.

(2) The idea of God is that of the most perfect being.

(3) But things which have much much less perfection than God (for example, minnows and criminals) exist.

(4) So God has much more existence than some things that exist.

(5) Therefore God exists.

Climacus objects to the first premise, saying that we must distinguish "ideal being" (that is, perfection) from "factual being" (for example, existence), noting that existence, unlike perfection, does not admit of degrees. No matter how perfect, wonderful, great, beautiful, moral, strong, happy, or wise something is, either it exists or it does not, and there is nothing more or less about it.

> With regard to factual being, to speak of more or less being is meaningless. A fly, when it is, has just as much being as the god; with regard to factual being, the stupid comment I write here has just as much being as Spinoza's profundity, for the Hamlet dialectic, to be or not to be, applies to factual being. Factual being is indifferent to the differentiation of all essence-determinants, and everything that exists participates without petty jealousy in being and participates just as much. (41f., note)

Climacus is surely right about being. The difficulty is that not all versions of the ontological argument depend on the silly assumption that there are degrees of existence. In particular St. Anselm's version in *Proslogion,* chapter two, does not. So perhaps we should take a look at a more eligible version of the argument before we concede to Climacus that belief in God cannot

---

[7]*Postscript,* 245.

be founded upon "understanding." An astute contemporary of ours, the logician/metaphysician Alvin Plantinga, claims to have formulated a sound, updated version of Anselm's argument. So I propose that we take a look at that.

Plantinga offers two statements of the argument, one of which is as follows:

> (42) There is a possible world in which unsurpassable greatness is exemplified.
>
> (43) The proposition *a thing has unsurpassable greatness if and only if it has maximal excellence in every possible world* is necessarily true.
>
> (44) The proposition *whatever has maximal excellence is omnipotent, omniscient, and morally perfect* is necessarily true.[8]

A few explanatory comments will clarify how the argument works. According to Plantinga there are a number of "great-making properties," properties that make things that have them great. For example, in a possible world in which Socrates is cowardly and avaricious, he is less great than he is in the actual world, in which he is courageous and unconcerned about money. But in a possible world in which he does not even exist, Socrates cannot have any excellences at all, and so he surely cannot be very great in such a possible world. Existence, then, while not itself a great-making property, is a necessary condition for greatness. So (42) in the above argument says that it is possible that God *exists;* for in a possible world in which God does not exist, he will not have any greatness at all, and so in that world, unsurpassable greatness will not be exemplified. But in a possible world in which unsurpassable greatness is exemplified, omnipotence, omniscience, and moral perfection are also necessarily exemplified, as (44) comments. Proposition 44 can be read as merely a rendering explicit of what is contained in the notion of unsurpassable greatness. Something else contained therein is made explicit in (43): The greatness of something in one possible world may be determined, according to Plantinga, not only by the properties it possesses in that world, but by properties it possesses in other possible worlds. In particular, unsurpassable greatness could be exemplified only by something that possessed its excellent-making properties (and, of course, existence would be a necessary condition therefor) in every possible world. (In other words, the notion that unsurpassable greatness is exemplified in some but not all possible worlds is incoherent.) If this principle is correct, then if it is possible that God does not exist (that is, if there is any possible world in which he does not exist) he necessarily does not exist; that is, he does not exist in *any* possible world. Conversely, if it is possible that God exists, then it is

---

[8]Alvin Plantinga, *The Nature of Necessity* (Oxford: Clarendon Press, 1974) 216.

necessary that he does; for it is possible that he exists only if he exists in every possible world. So it follows from premise 42 that God exists. If we grant that there is a possible world in which unsurpassable greatness is exemplified, then we must also grant that there is no possible world in which it is not exemplified.

To put the argument in a form that is even simpler (and also less transparent) than Plantinga's statement,

> (1) It is possible that God exists.
> (2) If it is possible that God exists, then he exists.
> (3) Therefore, God exists.

Now according to Plantinga, even though this argument is sound, it is not a *proof* of God's existence, since its main premise (42 above, or 1 here) is controversial. That it is possible that God exists looks superficially like a minimal acknowledgment, which even a committed atheist might concede. He might say "Sure, it's *possible* that God exists, but I'll bet my buttons that he doesn't" much in the same way a philosophical Kansan might say, on a scorching August morning, "I'll admit it's possible it'll rain today—but it won't." But if Plantinga is right, some reflection on the concept of God will show a person that (2) is true—indeed, just an elucidation of that concept. In that case, (1) begins to look considerably less innocuous, and the committed atheist will no doubt shift his ground and deny that it is (even) possible that unsurpassable greatness is exemplified.

So Plantinga does not claim to have proved the existence of God with his version of the ontological argument. He does claim that the argument shows that it is *rational* for a person to believe in God.[9] Climacus's ear should perk up at this, since it sounds like a challenge to his thesis that the canons of thought that he calls "the understanding" cannot provide grounds for believing in the god. This ontological argument, according to Plantinga, shows that belief in God is rational by showing that the conclusion "God exists" follows from a premise that a rational person can hold, namely that unsurpassable greatness is possibly exemplified. At the same time, however, he concedes that a rational person might accept other premises (for example, "Near-maximality is possibly exemplified"[10]) that yield the conclusion that God does *not* exist. What does he mean, then, by claiming that it is rational to accept his premise? Often when we claim that a belief is rational, we are claiming that there is a preponderance of considerations (evidence or at least pragmatic considerations) in its favor; that is, we are claiming that the belief

---

[9]See Alvin Plantinga, *God, Freedom, and Evil* (New York: Harper & Row, 1974) 112.

[10]See Plantinga, *The Nature of Necessity,* 218-19.

has "rational *support.*" But Plantinga does not claim that his argument shows belief in God to be rational in this sense, since it offers no reason for preferring his premise over other, antithetical ones, or to elect a suspension of judgment about it. So his argument does not show that belief in God is more reasonable than disbelief. He seems to mean just that a person commits no epistemic indiscretion in affirming the premise, nor any fallacy in drawing the conclusion from it.

What reason might a person have for thinking it's a good bet that unsurpassable greatness is possibly exemplified? As I noted, if somebody does not understand the implications of the premise, he will not think it commits him to much. So he might think it's a good bet just because he thinks it's an extremely minimal commitment. But then he would be wrong, and Plantinga is lurking in the shadows ready to ambush him with all the machinery of quantified modal logic. But if the thought that God exists horrifies him, he still has a rational way out of his fix; for he can simply decide that in view of its untoward implications, the premise must be abandoned. On the other hand, if he is a pro-God sort of person, he will probably like the premise precisely because of its implications. So a person might indeed have reasons for preferring Plantinga's premise to the antithetical ones, or vice versa—namely their theological implications. But is there any other reason for preferring the one to the others? I cannot see any and, it seems, neither can Plantinga.[11]

So despite the enormous logical superiority of Plantinga's argument over the piece of intellectual flotsam from Spinoza, we are still where Climacus said we are—namely without any argument that gives us a reason—even a noncompelling reason—for believing in God. It would be too much to accuse Plantinga's argument of committing the "leap" by embedding the belief in God in the premise set. The belief in God's existence is not in any sense *in* the premise set of that argument. But for someone who thoroughly thinks the argument through, it seems that there can be no reason for accepting the main premise as true other than a welcoming attitude toward the conclusion that is thereby ensured. So if the belief in God is not embedded in the premise, perhaps we should say it is *behind* the premise, as the only ra-

---

[11]One can imagine a situation in which Plantinga's argument makes it more rational for a person to believe in God. Consider the case of old mother Dykstra, a member of the Jarvis Christian Reformed Church. She is an unusual believer in that her belief in God is premised, in significant part, on the proposition that maximal greatness is possibly exemplified. Although she believes that God's existence follows from this premise, she hasn't the foggiest idea how it follows. One Sunday afternoon, when the coffee guests have departed, she snuggles down in a soft chair with a copy of *The Nature of Necessity,* and within an hour Plantinga's clarifications have upgraded the rationality of her belief in God.

tional motivation for accepting it. The argument itself in no way supports the belief in God.

I have suggested that Climacus's treatment of the teleological and ontological arguments is offered as evidence for the second premise in the argument outlined on page 65: that the god is unknowable to the understanding. For such a generalization, his sampling of the understanding's efforts is admittedly meager. Before accepting his generalization, one would want to survey carefully all the most plausible arguments that have been offered by philosophers in the past. Even then, one would have to admit that the generalization involved some hazarding; for the conclusion is not just that the god is unknown to the understanding, but that he is unknowable—implying that there cannot ever be a proof of the god's existence.

Furthermore, we should keep in mind a point made by George Mavrodes in his book *Belief in God:*[12] that proofs are person-relative, and so a proof need not prove God's existence to every sane and intelligent person. To qualify as a proof, all that is required of an argument is that it be sound (valid with true premises) and convincing to *someone.* For an argument to be convincing to a person, the person must know that the argument is sound and know the truth of its premises without inferring it from either the argument's conclusion or statements he knows only by inference from that conclusion.[13] That is, the argument has to be a possible source of knowledge of God to him. Many philosophers have thought that a proof needed to do more than this—namely to make God's existence undeniable to any sane and intelligent person. But Mavrodes's observations about the nature of proofs would allow us to admit as possible proofs arguments that could not meet this stringent requirement.

CLIMBING FOR A FALL

In the first section of this chapter we saw that the concept of understanding has more than one facet, and that some of these can be descried sporting about rather freely in chapter three of *Fragments.* "Understanding" is a name for the human capacities to argue and explain, and for the norms governing them—indisputably legitimate norms as well as questionable ones. Analogously, it is the name for the norms and associated compulsions of common sense—and again, for the fundamental passion of every individual to find a satisfactory way of thinking out his own existence. These aspects of the concept are obviously related in various ways. Notably, when technical reason is applied to the question of God's existence, the passion of the

---

[12]George Mavrodes, *Belief in God* (New York: Random House, 1970).

[13]Ibid., 34 and all of ch. 1.

subjective thinker is always somewhere in the background. If one of the norms of technical reason is the dubious one that we should never believe anything on insufficient evidence, then the failure of the proofs may arouse "passion" in two senses: as a technical reasoner the inquirer may be frustrated by his inability to get any light from "understanding" on the question, and as a subjective thinker he may be rendered anxious about his own life.

If we keep in mind the variety of facets that the understanding has in Climacus's discussion, most of the apparently wild, obscure, or even incoherent things he says can be seen to make sense and even to be true. However, the form in which these truths are delivered to us is that of the hilarious deduction. In the last five pages of the chapter (before the appendix), Climacus deduces that the understanding is seeking an encounter with the absolute paradox as the god who becomes man. How does the argument go? I think we can construe it initially as follows:

(1) The understanding, when it tries to prove the existence of the god, comes upon its limit as the unknown. (44) (That is, the proofs do not work.)

(2) "When the category of motion is replaced by the category of rest it is the different, the absolutely different." (44)

(3) "If a human being is to come truly to know something about the unknown (the god), he must first come to know that it is different from him, absolutely different from him." (46)

(4) Man's unlikeness to the god is sin. (47) But unlikeness is a relation and no relation can be known without knowing something about each of the terms of the relation. But one of the terms (viz. the god) is the unknown, so man cannot become aware of his sin on his own.

(5) Consequently, if the understanding is to be satisfied in its attempt to know the unknown, what is absolutely different from man must become like man in order that man may understand himself as absolutely different. That is, the god must become man.

This is the absolute paradox. "Thus the paradox becomes even more terrible, or the same paradox has the duplexity by which it manifests itself as the absolute—negatively, by bringing into prominence the absolute difference of sin and, positively, by wanting to annul this absolute difference in the absolute equality" (47). Nothing in the structure of this argument will be lost by removing the reference to sin, since "sin" is just the dogmatic name for the absolute unlikeness. So let's try to simplify the argument:

(1) The understanding desires to know the unknown.

(2) The unknown is the absolutely different.

(3) So the understanding desires to know the absolutely different.

(4) But the absolutely different cannot be known.

(5) Consequently, if what is absolutely different from man is to become known, then the absolutely different must become absolutely like man. But the absolutely different is the god, so it is the god who must become

man. But the absolutely different's becoming absolutely like is surely the absolute paradox.

Premise four is redundant, since we already have it from (2) that the absolutely unlike is unknown. (3) follows from (1) and (2). (1) is just a way of saying that people are interested, for one reason or another, in proving the existence of God apart from any appeal to authority or revelation, and that efforts to do this always fail; perhaps this is true—at any rate, let it pass. So (2) is the most questionable premise. What reason have we for accepting the identification of the unknown with the different?

Climacus suggests that the unknown and the different are two forms of the same concept, namely that of "the frontier that is continually arrived at [by the understanding]," (44) the different being this frontier under "the category of rest," the unknown being this same frontier under "the category of motion." Climacus suggests that this fact entitles us to infer that the god, being utterly unknown to the understanding (read "man"), is also utterly different from man, and that therefore if the god is ever to become known to man, he must also become like man.

This is suspect. It is not generally true that what is unknown to someone is therefore unlike that person. Identical twins, separated and kept in ignorance of each other, will certainly be unknown to each other; but this fact implies nothing about how similar they may be. Conversely, something's being different (from someone) does not imply that it is unknown (to him). All would agree, I think, that Jonas Salk is unlike the polio virus, but it does not follow that this virus is unknown to him. The concepts of unknownness and unlikeness lack the logical connection that Climacus seems to be attributing to them.

Maybe Climacus is thinking loosely, and does not intend that "the different" and "the unknown" are the static and dynamic forms of the same concept, but only that they are two descriptions of the same thing. It is true that there can be two descriptions of the same thing, between which there is no implication. "The pocket knife on the kitchen table" and "the gift my wife gave me for Father's Day" may well be descriptions of the same object, yet neither description implies the other. So maybe Climacus is only suggesting that "the unknown" and "the different" are two descriptions of the same thing—the god. But if this is so, then he cannot be offering the observation that they are two forms of the same concept as a reason for believing that since "the unknown" is a true description of the god, therefore "the absolutely different" is a true description of him too. For the one description does not imply the other. So Climacus still owes us a reason for believing that the god is utterly unlike man. But if the god is really the unknown, it is hard to see what reason he could give us for believing this.

So it looks as though premise two is being slipped in arbitrarily. That God is utterly different from man is certainly not self-evident, nor is this one of (or a summary of all) the characteristics traditionally predicated of God. (Omniscience and omnipotence, for example, are at least remotely analogous to human knowledge and power. Otherwise we would not understand these words at all.) Without the premise that the god is utterly unlike man, the conclusion towards which Climacus is driving the deduction—that the understanding, down deep, wants to encounter the paradox that the god who is absolutely unlike man has become man—evaporates.

If Climacus's premises were true, would his argument be sound? It seems not. To get to the conclusion that God must become man from Climacus's premises, we need yet another premise, to the effect that knowledge of God must be *complete;* partial knowledge is not knowledge at all in this case. If we assume, falsely, that things are unknown to man to the extent that they are unlike him, then it follows that if man is to have *complete* knowledge of God, God must become a man (that is, completely like man). It would not follow that if man is to have *some* knowledge of God, then God must become man. If, as Climacus's second premise would suggest, Salk understands the polio virus only to the extent of the tiny resemblance that exists between him and it, then it would seem that if God became as much like man as the virus is like Salk, man would be in a position to know *something* about God. But Climacus is no more willing than any other theologian I know of to assert that knowledge of God must be complete. So I conclude that the argument fails, not only because the second premise is false, but also because the argument is irreparably invalid.

THE LURE OF THE ABSOLUTE PARADOX

If the argument we have just examined is a piece of burlesque, what is Climacus's serious purpose? Designating Jesus as the absolute paradox is a striking way of calling attention to the dissonance that he creates in the minds and hearts of persons who know him more or less as persons in his own generation did. Our contemporaries, like those in Climacus's generation, have in various ways made Jesus easier to comprehend than he really is, and have thus created an illusion of faith where there is really no faith in him at all. The serious point of calling Jesus the absolute paradox is thus to correct the false impression of him that impedes a primitively Christian faith in him. It is a way of removing an obstacle to faith—the obstacle created by the well-meaning attempt to remove the essential obstacle to faith, which can be summarized as "the offense." Calling Jesus the paradox is strictly correlative to remarking upon the repelling effect that he has, when rightly met, on all who do not come to him in perfect faith. This, then, is one serious point in the ironical deduction of the absolute paradox.[14] But there are others.

The reader who labors, mystified but fascinated, over the details of this deduction of the absolute paradox will be drawn also to psychological insights that are woven into its fabric. For there are presented here some deep thoughts on the psychology of the pagan God-consciousness and upon its alteration in the Christian. First, the pagan.

> The paradoxical passion of the understanding is, then, continually colliding with this unknown, which certainly does exist but is also unknown and to that extent does not exist. The understanding does not go beyond this; yet in its paradoxicality the understanding cannot stop reaching it and being engaged with it. (44)

To interpret this passage we must appeal again to our distinction between the various facets of the concept of understanding. The pagan here is a subjective thinker, anxious about himself and eager to come to a heart-satisfying understanding of himself in a world in which the mutability of all visible things, including him, threatens to present itself as the final truth. Looking about him, he observes that the things that give his life its meaning—his family and friends, the physical objects in which he delights, the products of his mind and hands, and his own body—are all always at some stage in a process of either entering or leaving existence. His mind (or is it his heart? At any rate it's a facet of what we are calling "understanding") rebels at this picture of things. Something about it is rudely alien to some deep reaches of his nature. If what he sees before his eyes is the final truth, then, thinks his "understanding," there is something personally monstrous embedded in the essence of nature.

His mind, then, turns again and again to the idea of a benign eternality above, behind, or underneath the otherwise desperate flux. However vaguely, this idea (shall we call it a belief?) insistently permeates his experience of himself and the world. That it should do so seems almost to be a condition of his soul's surviving intact.

Now a second facet of "understanding" exerts itself, for like any judicious person he would have reasons for believing. He must have arguments

---

[14]Obviously the expression is also a dig at Hegel and his followers. Paradox, or conceptual antithesis, is what produces the "movement" in the Hegelian dialectic. There Jesus Christ, the God-man, is a stage in the process of the self-revelation of Absolute Spirit, in which all the paradoxes from along the way have been assimilated. Accordingly, Jesus would be a relative paradox, one we get beyond by resolving it. In calling Jesus the absolute paradox, then, Climacus is defying anyone who relativizes him in this way. Jesus is not a stage on the way to anything. He is the alpha and the omega, the Lord.

for the existence of this benign eternality, and reference to it must have its solid place in the explanation of other things. Furthermore, he would like to render more definite his idea of this being that so far is aptly characterized as the unknown. So he attempts to come to a knowledge of this unknown by way of investigation and argument, but the more rigorously he argues and investigates, the deeper and clearer becomes his despair of finding this incomparable treasure. Hence the verdict of technical reason is: The thing can't be done; forget it and go back to your wife and food and work.

But the subjective thinker in him is not so easily put off. He is obsessed by the idea of this unknown, lured almost as if by a beckoning voice calling from out of the depth of . . . himself? nature? calling him . . . home. The idea, the voice—call it what you will—pursues him and will not let him alone.

The concept of a benign eternality, vague as it otherwise may be, is the concept of something fundamentally unlike things visible. For the benign eternality is at least eternal, and nothing else *seems* to be so. Accordingly, the concept is not utterly opaque, as Climacus seems to suggest when he says that "it is the absolutely different in which there is no distinguishing mark" (44f). "Absolutely different" would here have to mean "not characterizable in any way—not even by way of contrast—with things that are known." But by my suggested criterion of unlikeness the benign eternality would not be "absolutely" different, since it could at least be characterized as not-perishing. So when in paganism the likes of Julius Caesar is confused with God, it is not "quite consistently" that the understanding [man] "confuses itself with the difference [the god]" (45). A person who has the concept of a benign eternality ought not to go thinking that Julius Caesar is it, since Caesar is neither eternal nor consistently benign.

Yet, as Climacus remarks, "In the realm of fantastical fabrication, paganism has been adequately luxuriant" (45). There is something akin to "the self-ironizing of the understanding" in the fact that the pagan who starts with the notion of a benign eternality should end up with gods who are such markedly finite and even nasty people. Anthropomorphism itself is not inappropriate, notwithstanding what Climacus seems to suggest when he characterizes the god (ironically, I think) as the absolutely different. For it is certainly not impossible that God is a mind something like a human person even though, in being eternal and benign, he is different from human persons.

What then is the explanation of the "fantastical fabrications" of paganism? Climacus says, "What, then, is the difference? Indeed, what else but sin?" (47) So when Climacus says that the understanding "cannot absolutely negate itself but uses itself for that purpose," (45) and "Adhering to the understanding, the difference has so confused the understanding that it does not know itself and quite consistently confuses itself with the difference,"

(45) he is giving, not a philosophical, Hegelian, deductive explanation of the fantastical fabrications, but a Christian dogmatic one (couched though it is in an alien vocabulary). People conceive God perversely not because nothing can be known of God by the understanding and consequently "anything goes in natural theology," but because their judgment, like other parts of their character, is perverted by sin. When Climacus says that the understanding "cannot absolutely transcend itself and therefore thinks as above itself only the sublimity that it thinks by itself," (45) his real view resembles that of John Calvin, who says, "Indeed vanity joined with pride can be detected in the fact that, in seeking God, miserable men do not rise above themselves as they should, but measure him by the yardstick of their own carnal stupidity, and neglect sound investigation. . . . They do not therefore apprehend God as he offers himself, but imagine him as they have fashioned him in their own presumption."[15]

The understanding is subject to the self-irony that when it sets out to make more definite the idea of a benign eternality (which naturally suggests itself to subjective thinking), it ends up contradicting what it knows about God and offering, often, ridiculous and deeply unedifying conceptions. In traditional language, this is because the understanding has been corrupted by sin. The thinker, being ambivalent about God, sabotages his own thinking about God as a way of perverse self-defense.

Having thus invented his gods, the pagan has also subverted his own religious need, since if God is anything, he must be something that no human being has invented. The pagan is also dissatisfied for another reason: Because of the demands of technical reason, he is not willing to leave his knowledge of God at the mere vague notion of a benign eternality for which his heart yearns. And yet he cannot seem to get beyond this. For every effort to do so, "At the very bottom of devoutness there madly lurks the capricious arbitrariness that knows it itself has produced the god" (45). Let us then assert these two propositions: (1) An adequate God-relationship assumes that the believer does not believe that he invented his God, and (2) God must be more definite to the believer than the mere notion of a benign eternality that is natural to the mind of the subjective thinker.

Perhaps we can now see that there is something religiously fitting in a relevation that in selected ways is incongruous with everyday human understanding (in particular with what I have called common sense). If the believer can come to rest satisfied in the belief that he has derived his more detailed knowledge of God *from God,* then the mad, anxious, and desperate caprice that he or some of his fellow human beings have invented God (what

---

[15]*Institutes,* 1:4:1.

a contradiction!) will have been quieted. Of course any conception of God can in principle be presented as a revelation, so something more is required if the believer is to gain some confidence that his understanding of God is really from God and not invented by man. Accordingly, the revelation will be more firmly believable if it bears the stamp of something that no eye has seen, nor ear heard, nor the heart of man conceived. It will need to look like something that was not dished up from the soup of mythology.

The suggestion that God became a poor and politically powerless carpenter-teacher who was eventually executed as a criminal would seem to qualify. The story's incongruousness to common sense is of course not the only feature of it that lessens the suspicion that it was rooted in mythology. Jesus behaves very much like the God of the prophets, both in his wrath and in his tender mercy, as well as in the authority with which he speaks. His resurrection from the dead is of course the crowning historical corroboration of his claimed identity. Still, the story's capacity to shock common sense is one of the things that recommends it as a veridical revelation. This, then, is another dimension of Climacus's claim (interpreted nonironically) that the understanding desires its own downfall:

> The "understanding" construed as the subjective thinker has a vague notion of a benign eternality without which his life is a monstrosity; but understanding construed as the reasonable demands for definiteness and groundedness of belief generates a dissatisfaction with this vague notion; but a person cannot undertake, on his own resources, to ground and further define his belief in God, because technical reason can by its nature yield no such results, and every attempt to make the belief more definite in *violation* of technical reason violates also the concept of belief in God, which demands that belief expel the suspicion that man has invented God. And one shape of answer to the dilemma thus posed is a revelation of God with elements of incongruity to understanding as "common sense."

THE REAL CHRIST

Thus the believer in Jesus Christ finds satisfaction of some of his deepest needs precisely in those features of the story that shock his "worldly" modes of thought. As a subjective thinker he is aware of the desperate bankruptcy of those modes of thought as a basis for self-understanding. As one who is clear that God cannot both be the object of belief and be conceived as possibly a human invention, he finds some confirmation for the objectivity of this revelation in its repugnancy to common sense.

The story that God in his love was born a man, one of the lower middle class without formal education, and that this man taught (consistently) that no one enters the favor of God but by him—this story is not what a reasonable, educated, liberal-minded person would expect from God. Common sense would perhaps admit that God reveals himself through human beings, that one can see reflections of him in them, and perhaps more reflection of him in some of them than in others. But the claim that one man not just reveals God but *is* God and that absolutely nobody else is will seem absurd. Common sense would expect a revelation of God to be ethically effective and politically potent; yet by this standard Jesus—who had no political power, did not even attempt to organize the masses, and ended in the ignominy of the cross—seems to be rather beside the point. Ethical common sense (not to be taken lightly, by the way) would have it that if we have failed morally, then the way to rectify the situation is to make amends for our misdeeds. If I am not righteous, the only way to become so is by a change of character; such common sense can only shake its head in dismay at the suggestion that *one* man can make amends for *all,* and that *my* righteousness before God consists in *his.* Consequently to a person who will not relinquish this common sense, Jesus Christ is offensive in a much more virulent way than the mere proposal to believe in God is. He precipitates a choice: either to hold on to common sense, or to adopt the Christian outlook, which takes as its central fact and point of departure the assertion that God did do this (to common sense) unreasonable thing.

In the appendix to chapter three, Climacus discusses the offense, though he does so in a manner that, surprisingly, does not emphasize the offensiveness, the repugnancy to common sense, of Jesus Christ.[16] Instead he makes a single point, driving it home again and again through these six pages. The point is that the understanding is passive and weak in relation to the paradox. He expresses this point in various ways, all of which are rather indications of his meaning than precise formulations: "No matter if the offense came and took the last crumb of comfort and joy from the offended one or if it made him strong—offense is nevertheless a suffering [that is, a passive attitude]" (50). "[O]ffense does not understand itself but is understood by the paradox" (50). "The understanding declares that the paradox is the absurd, but this is only a caricaturing" (52). "When the understanding cannot get the paradox into its head, this did not have its origin in the understanding but in the paradox itself" (53). "Is it not peculiar that the paradox thus seems to be taking bread from the mouth of offense and making it an unremunerative art?" (54)

---

[16]For a discussion of the offense that does lay emphasis on the offensiveness of Jesus, by an author closely associated with Climacus, see part two of *Practice in Christianity.* Also, for a lucid explanation of how three "species of thinking-man's reaction to the Paradox" are at bottom cases of offense, see H. A. Nielsen, *Where the Passion Is* (Tallahassee: University Presses of Florida, 1983) 89-99. Nielsen (89) asks the question I answer below, namely, "What is [Climacus's] stake in emphasizing the essential passivity of offense?" But he does not, as far as I can see, answer this question.

We have seen that the seriousness in chapter three of *Fragments,* once it is disentangled from the hilarious deduction of the absolute paradox, comes down to a series of insights, logical and psychological, concerning the relations between faith and "understanding." Perhaps it is worth summarizing those points here.

(1) God's existence is inscrutable to what we have called "technical reason," and consequently the hope or feeling of compulsion to establish his existence by argument is unedifying and an enemy of faith; Climacus would engender in his reader a healthy resignation to these facts.

(2) When a person searches for a way of understanding his own existence that will satisfy his deepest personal needs, he comes to realize that the common sense categories that tend to have natural sway over human beings are inadequate and some kind of positive relation to an eternal order of things is needed. Climacus once even goes so far as to say that there has never been an atheist. So what "understanding" in one sense cannot establish, "understanding" in another sense already knows, at least subconsciously as an object of yearning. Thus we have a partial explanation of the "paradoxical passion of the understanding."

(3) Belief in Jesus Christ involves the abandonment of some canons of common sense, and consequently the proposal to believe (if it is not watered down into something essentially non-Christian) will meet with offense on the part of people who refuse to abandon these canons.

(4) But also, this very "paradoxicalness" of the Christian claims about Jesus ministers to a human need, the need for a revelation of God about which the believer can confidently affirm that it did not arise in any human heart. And so Jesus Christ can be said to fulfill the understanding's desire for its own downfall—not only because he is the ground of that form of life that is ultimately satisfying to the subjective thinker in each of us (see (2) above), but also because there is something deeply congruent (even reasonable!) about his being at odds with common sense.

This last theme—that Jesus Christ in his "paradoxical" character addresses the potential believer as the Master himself, as the authoritative one whom not to love as savior is "the erroneous accounting, ... the conclusion of untruth" (51)—is the single point of the appendix and the sense of the passages quoted on page 86. Jesus, precisely as the alien intruder upon common sense, presents himself as the objective truth and thus as the index or criterion of truth (see p. 51). The case is different with the fawning, domesticated, unparadoxical Christs of "liberal" and "conservative" apologetics. The common-sense Christs, preached from many pulpits, who seek to capture our modern attention by speaking directly to our political and cultural needs, or by offering to help us cope with the familial, financial, and psychological pressures of our daily life, by contrast, do not present themselves as objective, authoritative, and lordly. The obsequious Christs whose "divinity" is proven by their utility in profoundly influencing human history and culture are in the same case as is the existentialist Christ whose function is (and whose entire being consists in) rousing the soul of the "believer" from the slumbers of inauthenticity.

All these Christs are more or less patent and transparent figments. Not only for their inventors, but also for those upon whom they are perpetrated, "at the very bottom of devoutness there madly lurks the capricious arbitrariness that knows it itself has produced the god" (45). Jesus of Nazareth, the man of history who claims to be God and Lord and offers himself upon the cross for the sins of the world, authenticates himself when he is humbly and rightly preached. He is not a product of theology, or hermeneutics, or church councils, or any such human thing. As the paradox and the offense against common human sense, he presents himself as the uninvented living Lord.

PART TWO

SURVEYING
THE HEIGHTS

CHAPTER 4

THE RELATIONSHIP OF THE CONTEMPORARY FOLLOWER

CHAPTER FOUR OF *FRAGMENTS* marks a stylistic, formal, and substantive shift. In a sense it is not until now that Climacus addresses the question of the title-page: "can an eternal happiness be built on historical knowledge?" For only now does he begin an explicit discussion of historical knowledge and events. Of course, in speaking of the god in time he has all along been referring to a historical point of departure for an "eternal happiness." But a discussion of the historical judgment in which a person becomes conscious of having been recreated by the god has been deferred until a number of basic things have been laid out (indirectly) via the hilarious (and sometimes reckless) deductions of chapters one through three. So, appropriately, Climacus has coyly refrained from naming the happy passion of mutual understanding and love between the "teacher" and the disciple, which he now names "faith."

Another difference that sets off chapters four and five from the earlier ones is a kind of dialectical relaxation.[1] The heavy-handed deductions of the first three chapters are replaced by a more casual and desultory mode of exposition. Indeed, these chapters can be read as a series of grammatical remarks, somewhat repetitive and loosely hung together, which serve to sketch the similarities and differences between Christian faith on the one side and all other historical beliefs on the other.

This is not to say that Climacus has abandoned his irony and taken up direct discourse for the remainder of his book. Even though he does no more deducing to speak of in these last two chapters, he keeps up the pretense that what he has achieved so far has been achieved as results of the thought experiment. Consequently his grammatical remarks are embedded in an

---

[1]Paralleling the dialectical relaxation is a relaxing of the emotional tension between Climacus and his interlocutor. By the time we get to their last conversation, their harmony is so complete that Climacus answers, "Very eloquently spoken, I would say, if modesty did not forbid me, for you speak as I myself would speak" (105).

ironical context, and this fact has some obvious consequences for their mode of expression. But even without the distorting influence of the thought experiment, Climacus is capable of ironically formulated grammatical remarks. The *Concluding Unscientific Postscript* has an extremely desultory style, and also is concerned with sketching the boundaries of Christian thought and life, with a view to heading off conceptual and psychological vagrancy in that sphere. But his grammatical remarks there have a peculiar density and outrageousness of formulation that force the reader to appropriate the point for himself by returning with it to the primitive Christian and personal context—on pain of becoming the butt of a Climackean joke. Examples of such remarks are "Christianity is not a doctrine" (339), "God does not exist, he is eternal" (296), and "Truth is subjectivity" (169ff.). To read such remarks as more or less straightforward theoretical points of epistemology or metaphysics implying that, for example, the teachings of Christianity must be reinterpreted as noncognitive, that God is not a being but radical transcendence, and that in religious matters the categories of true and false must be replaced by those of committed and uncommitted, would be to fall victim to the Climackean "irony" in a way closely analogous to that of the person who reads the hilarious deductions of chapters one through three with a straight face. To avoid this embarrassment we must read such remarks as incitements to grammatical thought.

Climacus uses the word "faith" in a narrow and specifically Christian way in these last chapters. A mere belief in God, even if filled with pathos and a sense of responsibility to him, is not faith in this sense (see 87). Socrates, though he had a God-relationship, and Abraham, though he was willing to sacrifice Isaac if God required it, did not have faith in this sense. Of course the loose way in which people sometimes speak of the faith of a Buddhist, Hindu, or Stoic—or even of an existentialist—is something entirely other. Faith, in Climacus's present sense, is a "paradoxical" coalescence of historical affirmation with a trusting and grateful love of God. It is that "happy passion" (59) in which the believer construes the man Jesus of Nazareth as the Lord of the universe and the Lamb of God that takes away the sins of the world.

The notion that a person's relationship to God (the eternal) should have as its necessary condition the occurrence of a historical event or sequence of historical events seems absurd to common religious sense. To this common sense (of which Climacus tells us that Socratic thinking is the crowning achievement), the question of what has occurred historically and the question of what the conditions are for a person's coming into a right relationship with God, are questions belonging to mutually exclusive categories. No answer to the one kind of question can be an answer to the other. So the Christian assertion that each person's God-relationship is conditioned by his or her relation to a particular historical personage who lived according to particular customs in a particular culture at a particular place and time, seems paradoxical.[2] And the life of the believer, characterized by the passion described above, likewise seems paradoxical. Not that it makes no sense at all (quite to the contrary); but the sense it makes is not common, not natural, not something that would have been likely to arise in the heart of any human being.

Climacus spends chapter four remarking about various features of this unnatural but happy passion, limiting himself for the most part to the case of the disciple who is historically contemporary with Jesus Christ. He will devote chapter five to considering whether faith may have some special features in the case of historically subsequent individuals who must therefore depend on testimony.

Climacus points out repeatedly that there is no way for a contemporary of Jesus to "see" that Jesus is God and savior with the physical eyes, since Jesus' magnificence is "something not to be seen immediately" (66). Neither can Jesus' identity and accomplishment be inferred (by the help of warrants from technical reason or common sense) from what he does and undergoes.

Climacus also suggests that certain features of Jesus' life-history are signs of his identity and saving work, neither more nor less:

> The god did not, however, take the form of a servant in order to mock human beings; his aim, therefore, cannot be to walk through the world in such a way that not one single person would come to know it. Presumably he will allow

---

[2]Thus Climacus expresses himself: "but the paradox specifically unites the contradictories, is the eternalizing of the historical and the historicizing of the eternal" (61). If one reads this sentence out of context, it is natural to construe it, not as the paradox I have described above, but as an implicit technical contradiction. Thus one might think, "The eternal is what is timeless or outside of time, and the historical is necessarily in time. Thus for something that is eternal to become historical is for something that is timeless to take on temporal characteristics. But this is not like the "paradox" of something gaining a characteristic that *habitually* it does not have, as when we obtain a paradoxical gerbil by dyeing him purple. For the eternal is *essentially* nontemporal. That is, if it becomes temporal it *eo ipso* ceases to be the eternal. So it is a technical contradiction to say that the eternal was made historical." But this is a misreading of Climacus's sentence. It is clear in the context that "the eternal" implies nothing one way or the other about the "temporality" of God, unless it be that if God lived for thirty or so years in our time, then his nature must be such that he can live in time without ceasing to be God. "The eternal" is a cipher for God or the God-relationship; so to say that the historical was made eternal is to say that something historical came to be a necessary condition for people's God-relationship, and to say that the eternal became historical is just to say that God became man. This is a uniting of the "contradictories" not in the sense that the predicates are technically incompatible, but in the sense that their uniting boggles or offends commonsense ways of thinking about the relation between God and history.

> something about himself to be understood, although any accommodation
> made for the sake of comprehensibility still does not essentially help the per-
> son who does not receive the condition . . . and it may just as well alienate the
> learner as draw him closer. (56)

These indications of Jesus' identity as the son of God and of his role as the lamb of God are recorded in the Gospels. Let us be a bit less algebraic than Climacus and look at a sampling of them. Jesus said to a paralytic, "My son, your sins are forgiven." The implied claim was not lost on the scribes who were sitting there: "It is blasphemy! Who can forgive sins but God alone?" (Mark 2; see also Luke 7). It is hard to miss the parallel between Jesus' feeding five thousand hapless people in a wilderness place (Mark 6) and Jah-weh's feeding manna to the children of Israel in the desert (Exod. 16). When, a little later, Jesus demonstrates his power over wind and water, the disciples are astounded, and Mark explains their surprise by saying, "they did not understand about the loaves, but their hearts were hardened." When, in his pronouncement (and even revision) of the law, Jesus uses the formula, "You have heard that it was said. . . . But I say to you" (Matt. 5), he seems to be speaking the law of God on his own authority, not like the scribes, or even like the prophets. A man who says the following seems to lack Socratic humility, to say the least: "All things have been delivered to me by my Father; and no one knows the Son except the Father, and no one knows the Father except the Son and any one to whom the Son chooses to reveal him. Come to me, all who labor and are heavy laden, and I will give you rest" (Matt. 11). Repeatedly Jesus predicted that he would be rejected and killed, and then would rise from the dead (Mark 8:31, 9:9, 9:31). When he went to Jerusalem for the last time, one of his first acts was to go to the Temple, the seat of God. Then, acting as though he was boss there, he cleansed it of impure elements and established it as his teaching headquarters (Mark 11). The audacity of this takeover, along with the accumulated offense of his words and actions, incited the religious establishment to take actions leading to Jesus' cruci-fixion as a criminal. After an interval of a couple of days he began appearing alive to various disciples on various occasions, and this continued for a few weeks (1 Cor. 15:3-7, Luke 24).

When Climacus calls this teacher "a human being in a lowly form who said of himself that he was the god," (93) he is speaking somewhat in the retrospective manner of the Gospel of John, which attributes to Jesus ver-bally explicit claims to be the son of God, very different in style from the synoptic Gospels. The difference here is essentially one of directness of style, and not a difference of claim; for Jesus' actions and words as recorded in the synoptics make less directly the same claim as the one that John ex-presses in the words, "I and the Father are one" (10:20).

To say that these historical features are signs of Jesus' identity, neither more nor less, is to say two things. First, to ascribe to Jesus the identity and mission that Christians ascribe to him is not an arbitrary interpretation, a leap in the dark, a groundless and irrational ascription. It is not absurd to say that Jesus is the son of God and savior in the same way that it would be to pick somebody at random from the Cincinnati telephone directory and ascribe this identity and mission to him.[3]

Second, they are not *more* than signs. Even if there is no such thing as brute perception, there is still a place for the distinction between "direct" perception and "interpretation," and Climacus is saying that to take Jesus as the son of God falls in the latter category. The concept of direct apprehension has fuzzy boundaries and shifting application, as we should expect of a concept correlative with that of common sense. The "sense" that is common to one group of people may be strange to another and, correlatively, what one group perceives directly requires from the other an interpretive act.

Let us say that some children are torturing a kitten—pulling its tail, dunking it in water, and sticking pins in it—-and thoroughly enjoying themselves. Possibly they do not see their activities as wicked. It is not that they think what they are doing is morally good or neutral; moral categories are simply not in play for them. An adult comes along and sees, without either interpretation or inference, that the children are behaving wickedly. If you ask him, "Did you perceive the children's activity as immoral?" he will perhaps answer (especially if he is neither a philosopher nor a psychologist), "What do you mean "perceive *as*? There's no other way to see it." Now he begins to lecture the children: "How would you like somebody to dunk you in water and stick pins in you, just to see you gasp and scream?" Some of the children will perhaps laugh at him, or run away and hope to resume their activity out of sight; but others will be willing to see, with his provocation, what they did not see on their own.

These latter children may be genuinely engaged in the activity of interpretation of their actions. They do not naturally and directly perceive the wickedness, but they are able, with interpretive aids, to see their activity as wicked. The transition from seeing-as (interpretation) to direct seeing is an important part of moral and religious education. Direct seeing is the goal, but the transition to it is characterized by interpretation. For the children who are in this stage of transition, or for someone reflecting on the matter from the angle of this transition, the fact that the children are intentionally distressing the kitten might be called a "sign" that evil is being done—-that is, it is a datum that lends itself to a moral interpretation.

---

[3]See Climacus's remarks on such a possibility, 45-46.

When Climacus suggests that certain features of Jesus' life history are not more than signs of his identity and mission, he is looking at the matter, so to speak, in the context of conversion, of that time in the believer's life when he is *becoming* a Christian but has not yet been fully gripped by the happy passion. To a fully mature Christian it would indeed seem odd to describe Jesus' life as constituted only of signs of his identity: for the fully mature believer's consciousness is not like that of the child who is able to interpret sticking pins in a kitten as evil, but like the mature moral person who simply sees that this activity is immoral. The fully mature Christian's consciousness cannot be described as seeing (or interpreting) Jesus as his savior (though a thoroughly converted apostle could presumably have enough empathy with the partially converted to describe for their sakes some of the more striking features of Jesus' story as clues or indicators).

So Climacus is making a broad generalization about pre-Christian common sense: No kind of common sense that naturally grows up among humans will perceive Jesus directly as Lord and savior. In fact, every kind of common sense other than that engendered by the Holy Spirit will greet with offended puzzlement the suggestion that this man is God incarnate, come to atone for the sins of the world. For these common senses, then, the features of Jesus' life history will have the status of not more than signs, fully as capable of alienating the learner as of drawing him closer (56).

The analogy between Christian faith as a historical affirmation and historical affirmations that are more or less directly deliverable to common sense can easily mislead a person to think that he would have faith if he knew just a little more about the historical Jesus. No doubt something can be known "directly" about Jesus, since like anything else historical, Jesus' life and death are in principle subject to mastery in the common-sense manner of a newspaper reporter or a historical scholar. But about this Climacus sets the grammar straight by remarking that "knowing a historical fact—indeed, knowing all the historical facts with the trustworthiness of an eyewitness— by no means makes the eyewitness a follower" (59).

What is it to be a disciple, then? In Climacus's word it is to be "contemporary" with Jesus Christ. Climacus teases the reader with equivocation on this term in phrases like "despite his being contemporary, a contemporary can be a noncontemporary; the genuine contemporary is the genuine contemporary not by virtue of immediate contemporaneity" (67). In the sense in which faith is contemporaneity with Jesus Christ, contemporary means "spiritually present"; faith is a state of communion or presence with the son of God. This presence is mediated historically, either by "immediate contemporaneity" such as the apostle Peter enjoyed or by a historical report. Climacus's point in the above quote is that the spiritual communion with Christ, which passionately construes this historical figure as Lord and savior, is not guaranteed by such things as watching Christ heal a paralytic and forgive his sin or confirming the report of this even with the greatest possible certainty. Someone might know a great many such things with a high degree of certainty without Christ's becoming "present" to him in this spiritual sense; conversely, someone who knew very little about the historical Jesus might, by construing him as his God and redeemer, enjoy to the full this spiritual contemporaneity with Christ.

There is no proposition, either in common sense or in technical reason, that will warrant the inference that since Jesus forgave sins, spoke with authority, healed diseases, cast out demons, succored the outcast, was crucified, and rose from the dead, he is the son of God and the savior of the world. For such an inference to be valid, one would need, in addition to the facts of this man's life, a principle to the effect that when a person lives a life like this, he is (or is probably) the son of God. Of course no such principle exists in technical reason or common sense. So if one attempts to reason from the "indicators" of Jesus' identity to the conclusion that he is God and savior, the assertion will be based on a fallacy. But even if one could reason to this conclusion, the reasoning would not give one faith, since faith is not just an assertion, even a well-grounded one, but a passion, and the passion would certainly not be guaranteed by the fact of going through the argument.

How then does faith relate to the elements of the story, what I have called the "signs"? We might be inclined to think that since faith is neither a simple grasping of the historical facts, nor a conclusion from them, it must be a decision with regard to them. One simply *decides* to *take* Jesus as one's Lord and savior, simply performs the act of construing him in that way. There is something to recommend this analysis of the situation, but this too would violate the grammar of faith. Climacus says again and again that the god must provide the condition (namely faith), and he says flatly, "faith is not an act of will" (62). The construal of Jesus as Lord and savior, the happy passion by which one sees in him the ground of one's peace with God is, by the very logic of the case, not something a person can do on his own.

I say "by the very logic of the case" because this remark is not based on introspection or psychology. I do not ask myself what the conversion experience was like, and then inevitably describe it in passive terms: "The Holy Spirit just came and took me by the soul and claimed me for his own; I felt as though I was being *dragged* to the altar; I was *possessed.*" The experience of conversion is not universally this, and even if it were, there would be a deeper reason for attributing faith to the working of God in one's heart. For what is faith? It is a love relationship with God through Jesus Christ. But who is Jesus Christ? He is the atonement for one's sins. So faith is the passionate acknowledgment that apart from Jesus one is without hope, lost and alienated from God—so deeply mired in sin that no action on one's own part, not even a responsive one, can establish this new relationship. Part of faith—determined by the fact that the object of faith is the lamb, which uniquely heals the breach between God and the believer—is the belief that the believer is without the condition even for construing Jesus as that lamb. So even if, at the moment of conversion, it looks phenomenologically as though one had, at least partially, by effort come to faith, still one corrects this judgment retrospectively by a dogmatic standard: God is entirely the author of one's faith. From within the perspective (the happy passion) of faith the ultimate ground of faith is seen to be not historical facts or reasoning about them or insight into them or any act of will concerning them, but a kind of authoritative testimony that is at the same time the irresistible personal intimacy of love, as though in the historical person Jesus or through the words of the narrative about him, God himself is whispering to the believer, "I love you; this is for you."

So the happy disposition to see Jesus as my Lord and savior is a gift of God. As Climacus remarks, this does not mean that the life of faith is a passive life, or that it involves no willing, for "once the condition is given, that which was valid for the Socratic is again valid" (63). The person who sees himself, dispositionally, as reconciled to God through Jesus Christ, may very well fail, in this or that situation, to construe himself as so redeemed. He may be envious of his colleagues over inessential matters such as advancement, scholarly accomplishment, and prestige. He may look upon the elderly people in his life as impediments to his freedom rather than as children of God, opportunities for sacrificial love, and flesh of his own flesh. He may fall into comparing himself, as to righteousness before God, with others, and into taking comfort in the observation that he is better than the average Christian. Such failures as these may even lead to a certain paralysis of spirit in which he becomes barely capable of the episodic construal of Jesus as Lord and lamb. In all of this he may not cease to believe (that is, to be willing to affirm Christianity), and so to believe that he has been *given* the condition. As Climacus says, the Socratic principle applies, namely, the principle that since he lives by the Spirit, he can be exhorted to walk by the Spirit, to work out his salvation in fear and trembling. Within the context of dispositional faith, then, it is fully appropriate to struggle to achieve faith, to deploy strategies for the deepening of faith, and to take responsibility for failures to construe the world as a Christian ought.

INTERLUDE

INTRODUCTION
TO THE INTERLUDE

THE INTERLUDE BETWEEN CHAPTERS FOUR AND FIVE is a defense of a thesis concerning historical beliefs in general. Thus it is in keeping with the two surrounding chapters, whose purpose is to delineate the grammar of that one particular historical belief that is Christian faith. Yet it is not directly a part of that grammatical inquiry, and so it is appropriate that it not be numbered among the chapters of the book. It is similar to an "aside" in a Shakespearean play—helpful but less than essential to the discussion, and delivered in a markedly different tone of voice from the chapters between which it is sandwiched.

Is the Interlude to be taken as a serious attempt at philosophy, or should we read it, as we have the hilarious deductions of chapters one through three, as a design to get us thinking? There is evidence on both sides, and I admit that I cannot decide between them. Had the Interlude been written by almost any other author, we would not doubt that it was meant straightforwardly. Further, in the introductory paragraph Climacus jokes with his reader in such a way as to prepare him to take the content of the Interlude seriously: the purpose of the section, says Climacus, is to create the illusion that 1,843 years have elapsed between chapter four and chapter five.

> Therefore, if you find me rather prolix, repeating the same thing "about the same thing," you must, please note, consider that it is for the sake of the illusion, and then you presumably will forgive me my prolixity and account for it in a far different and more satisfying way than to presume that I let myself think that this matter definitely required consideration, yours as well, inasmuch as I suspected you of not fully understanding yourself in this regard. (72)

The natural interpretation of this remark is to take it as ironical and thus the body of the Interlude as straightforward. As though Climacus is spoofing the reader in telling him that the present discussion is prolix and obvious and designed merely to create an illusion, whereas the discussion is in fact tight, unobvious, and philosophically serious.

But it would not be out of character for Climacus to pull a double irony on us. It is true that the Interlude is "tight"—indeed it is in the lecturing style of a professor of philosophy (and this ought to arouse a little suspicion as to its seriousness straightaway). Its difficulty is akin to that of the deductions of the first three chapters. So maybe the transparent irony of beginning the section by misdescribing it as frivolous is itself an irony obscuring the frivolousness of the heavy-handed philosophical content of the section. Furthermore, our analysis will reveal a pattern here that we have seen in parts of the book that we know to be ironical, namely that of stating (or suggesting) a truth, even a very simple one, but arriving at that truth by poor arguments, or couching the truth so obscurely that each reader must think his way to it on his own. In the past we have seen that the reckless arguments are a maieutic ladder by which the reader is induced to mount up to the truth for himself, eventually disposing of the ladder as an essential part of the process of assimilating the truth. On the other hand, against the supposition that the arguments of the Interlude are ironical, there is in the Interlude no internal literary evidence, like that of the dialogues in chapters one and two, that the arguments are not to be taken at face value.

So I think we cannot just decide how Climacus wants us to read his arguments. Of course, we do not need to, either. Maybe an irresolvable ambiguity of intention is more serviceable to Climacus than the more transparent ironies of other parts of the book. For it incites us even more nervously to think through his assertions for ourselves, and frees us to come, like Socrates's pupils, to the truth by virtue of our own hard labor. Accordingly I shall proceed as though I have no firm conviction how seriously Climacus intends his arguments; I shall simply adjudicate them according to the light that is in me.

The philosophical point of the Interlude is, as I said, a general thesis about historical beliefs. The proposal is that such beliefs cannot be known with objective certainty, but can only be believed by virtue of an act of will. As a claim about all historical beliefs, this thesis is strongly counterintuitive. Consider just two typical historical beliefs for now. I believe that I ate All Bran for breakfast this morning, and I believe that Thomas Jefferson was influential in early American politics. The first belief is very firm because it happened recently and is a fact over which I presided, and I am sound of mind and not at all in the habit of making mistakes about such things. The belief about Jefferson is uninfected with objective uncertainty because it is hedged by unspecificity and is one the denial of which would require the revision or elimination of thousands of beliefs about American history that are either certainly true or very likely candidates for truth. We seem to hold many historical beliefs with considerable objective certainty, and we do not notice, at any rate, performing acts of will in connection with all our historical beliefs. Indeed, Climacus's thesis is sufficiently outrageous, *prima facie,* to elicit the suspicion that he has tongue in cheek. The thesis cries out for "interpretation."

The argument goes something like this: Truths can be known with certainty in two ways only—either by rational insight or by direct observation. If they can be known by rational insight, they must be necessary truths (either logically or causally necessary). Historical events do not happen with necessity, however, so propositions claiming the occurrence of them cannot be known by rational insight. How about direct observation, then? Surely historical truths can be known in principle with empirical certainty, at least by an eyewitness? No, says Climacus, and the reason is this: Historical assertions by eyewitnesses are composite, being first the assertion of some empirical datum (which can be known with certainty) and secondly the assertion that the event of which the datum is a datum has come into existence. This latter part of the assertion cannot be grasped directly by the senses, but must be affirmed by an act of the will. It follows that historical beliefs are objectively underdetermined. They cannot be known with certainty, though they can be held with certainty as essentially passionate resolutions.

So the Interlude is organized as a refutation of two theses: First, that the truths of history are necessary truths; and second that they are knowable by the direct deliverances of the senses. Roughly one half of the Interlude is devoted to each of these theses. In the next three sections I shall examine Climacus's discussion of these theses; and then I shall endeavor to reinterpret Climacus's general thesis about historical knowledge in the light of the deficiencies present in his discussion, and to see what bearing a cleaned-up version of his thesis might have on our account of the grammar of Christian faith.

ARE HISTORICAL TRUTHS
LOGICALLY NECESSARY?

In the first three sections of the Interlude Climacus seeks to disqualify the thesis that historical truths are necessary and can thus be known with the kind of certainty with which we can know some necessary truths. Historical truths are about events, and events are characterized by having *come into existence.* So he begins by asking, "What is the change (κίνησις) of coming into existence?" (73). Coming into existence is a peculiar kind of change, if indeed it is a kind of change at all. For change is always attributed to something, something that is supposed to have survived the change. Thus a tidy house can change into a shabby one only on condition that the same house that formerly was tidy has become shabby. Coming into existence seems not to meet this condition, since before something came into existence it did not exist. That is, the thing that takes on the predicate of existing does not seem to be anything at all, and so is not anything that is capable of taking on the predicate of existing.

When we hear the words "coming into existence" we probably think of dramatic examples such as the conception of a new human being or the construction of a new building. But for our present metaphysical purposes any state of affairs can be said to come into existence. The state of affairs consisting of the fourteenth ballpoint ever owned by R. C. Roberts running out of ink (let us call it ø) once came into existence. Now if this state of affairs' coming into existence is an example of change, what is the subject of this change—that is, what underwent the change of coming into existence? One might think that what underwent the change was the state of affairs immediately prior in time to ø, namely the state of affairs consisting of the fourteenth ballpoint ever owned by R. C. Roberts being on the verge of running out of ink (let us call it ψ). That is, ψ changed into ø. This last statement is no doubt true, but it is not an answer to our question. The question is, What is it that, taking on the predicate of *existence,* yields the state of affairs ø? ψ's taking on the predicate of existence will certainly not yield ø. If ψ already exists, it cannot take on existence; if it does take on existence, the state of affairs yielded is not ø but ψ.

Climacus's answer to this problem is that what takes on the predicate of existing or being actual is the *possibility* of the state of affairs that comes into existence. The possibility of the state of affairs exists (as it were) before it is actualized, and so qualifies as a candidate for that which underwent the change from nonexistence (nonactuality) to existence. So possibilities can be actualized or left unactualized, and when they are actualized it is they that undergo the change of coming into existence.

Now Climacus asks, "Can the necessary come into existence?" (74). To clarify this question, we must first ask what Climacus means by "the necessary." We can best approach this question by saying something about necessary truths, since necessity as a predicate of truths is more transparent than necessity as a predicate of predicates of things. Although Climacus couches his discussion in terms of "the necessary," "the historical," and so forth, his argument is ultimately about the conditions of our knowing historical truths, or holding historical beliefs. Here are some examples of necessary truths. "Seven plus five equals twelve." "If [(if the moon is made of green cheese then it is edible) and the moon is made of green cheese] then the moon is edible." "Circles lack angles." The mark of a necessary truth is, as its name implies, that it cannot be false. There are no circumstances, imaginable or otherwise, in which any of these propositions could be false. Though Climacus is not explicit on this point, it is this kind of necessity (what philosophers call "logical necessity") that he has in mind in most of his discussion.

There is another kind of necessity, which we might call factual necessity, that some propositions have. An example would be "No human being will ever fly to the moon without a mechanical aid." Though it is highly unlikely that this proposition will ever be falsified, it is false to say that there are no circumstances, imaginable or otherwise, in which it might turn out false. For example, humans can be imagined to evolve legs as powerful as any presently available rocket motor, along with a system for conserving oxygen and a skin capable of sustaining a simulated atmospheric pressure, and so forth. So the above proposition does not have necessary truth in the relevant sense.

Something important to notice, in the present context, about necessary truths is that they can often be known with perfect certainty. For a person who has a minimal mastery of the concepts employed in the three necessary truths mentioned in the preceding paragraph, it is impossible to doubt their truth. However, not all necessary truths are transparent and indubitable, or indeed even known. Alvin Plantinga mentions some propositions in mathematics—the Axiom of Choice, the Continuum Hypothesis, Goldbach's Conjecture, and Fermat's Last Theorem—which though either necessarily true or necessarily false are not known to be the one or the other.[1] Further, it is certainly possible for a person to be persuaded by fallacious reasoning that he knows something as a necessary truth when in fact he does not know it at all (in case it is not a truth). Still some necessary truths are transparent, and when we confront a proposition that is both transparent and necessary, we can affirm its truth with the highest degree of certainty.

So Hegel's philosophy of history, according to which historical truths are necessary in something like[2] the logical sense of 'necessary,' might seem to give grounds for thinking that we can know historical truths with the same kind of certainty with which we know that seven plus five equals twelve. Somebody who knows that seven plus five equals twelve not on anybody else's authority, but by mastering the logically necessary connections be-

---

[1]See Alvin Plantinga, *The Nature of Necessity* (Oxford: Clarendon Press, 1974) 5.

[2]Though Climacus obviously has Hegel in mind in this discussion, he does not explicitly attribute to Hegel the thesis that historical truths are necessary. His reason, perhaps, is that it is unclear whether Hegel held historical truths to be necessary in precisely the sense of 'necessary' that Climacus examines. The unclarity is not Climacus's fault but Hegel's, who never gives a satisfactory clarification of the thesis that history is the concrete outworking of logic (the Notion). So Climacus feels justified in assuming a fairly clear traditional notion of necessity in his discussion. (See Climacus's footnote [78] and a portion of the draft of *Fragments* not used in the book, *Journals and Papers,* II, # 1606.)

tween the concepts in the system of arithmetic, knows a necessary truth and knows it as necessary, that is, knows it by rational insight. Similarly, so goes the Hegelian story, a person who surveys history from the perspective (or nonperspective, as it were) of absolute knowledge, in which he sees the necessary connections between all things, would be able to know, for example, the truth "God was in Christ reconciling the world to himself" as a necessary truth, and thus without any of the dubiety that normally attaches to the affirmation of historical propositions.

Let us return now to Climacus's question: "Can the necessary come into existence?" The proposal that Hegel seems to be making—that events occur by logical necessity—is indeed very strange. So strange that one might be inclined to think of his entire construction of historical events and movements as a colossal grammatical joke if there were even the slightest hint that it ought to be taken that way. It is hard to know even how to begin to approach such a suggestion. The necessity by which it is impossible that a circle should have angles just is not a force by which things happen or fail to happen. Possibilities can be actualized, but necessities cannot. Possibilities are such things as that a water-burning engine will someday be invented, that the earth will be depopulated by a nuclear war, that suffering will some day end, that the Shah of Iran will be raised from the dead, and so forth. These are possibilities that can be actualized, and the corresponding propositions will become true if and only if they are actualized. But what would it be for seven plus five equals twelve to become actual? It is already true, without anything at all having to happen. Even to say that it is already true is misleading, for the category of time does not apply to it at all. To suggest that something might happen with respect to it would be the profoundest category mistake. It is, as it were, the eternal, and as Climacus says, "only the eternal has absolutely no history" (76).[3] "Coming into existence is a change, but since the necessary is always related to itself and is related to itself in the same way, it cannot be changed at all" (74). "Necessity stands all by itself. Nothing whatever comes into existence by way of necessity, no more than necessity comes into existence or anything in coming into existence becomes the necessary" (74). Climacus seems to be right on target with these grammatical remarks. Propositions about historical events are never true by logical necessity, and propositions expressing logical necessities never express possibilities, if we mean by possibilities states of affairs that can become actual. It can become true that the Shah of Iran is raised from the dead. It cannot become true that he will either be raised from the

---

[3]The Hong translation corrects a false lead in the Swenson translation. Without warrant from the Danish, Swenson capitalized the "e" in eternal here, suggesting that the referent is divine.

dead or he will not.[4] Consequently any hope of knowing historical truths with
the kind of certainty with which one can know transparent logical truths is
vain, being based on an outrageous confusion of these two spheres.

ARE HISTORICAL TRUTHS
CAUSALLY NECESSARY?

Attributing logical necessity to historical events is a confusion. But isn't
it still possible to attribute causal necessity to them? If causal necessity were
correctly predicable of historical events, then again it would seem to be in
principle possible to know them with perfect certainty. I say "in principle,"
because it is unlikely that any human would ever have enough information
actually to know anything historical in this way. The meteorologist is able
to predict weather events by knowing two things: the present weather facts
and the natural laws governing changes from one state of the weather to the
next. Meteorologists are humble people, and rightly so; they speak only of
degrees of probability of tomorrow's rain, and hedge their predictions even
more cautiously for next week or next year. They are cautious not because
the weather only roughly follows patterns and therefore in principle cannot
be predicted with certainty and precision. Their humility is based on ac-
knowledging their own imperfect grasp of the weather facts and weather laws.
It is assumed that a person who had a perfect control of these two kinds of
things would be able to make predictions accurate down to the last rain-
drop, down to the shape of each individual snowflake and the precise location and last millisecond of its contacting the earth (provided that no
human beings or other free agents were around casting monkey wrenches
into the works).

Maybe history is as we assume the weather is, only enormously more
complex. Perhaps every event, including every human action, is determined
in the following way: For every event that happens, there is a set of antecedent conditions such that if that set of conditions is actual, then the event
in question could not have not happened. Thus, if a person had a complete
mastery of the set of antecedent conditions, and also a complete grasp of

---

[4]Climacus is also obviously right in his insistence (76ff.) that whether a truth is
necessary or contingent has nothing to do with whether it is expressed in the past
tense. 'Socrates was wise' is true and immutably so; but not, therefore, necessarily
so in the logical sense. The unalterability of the truth value of this proposition is very
different from the unalterability of the truth value of "The interior angles of a triangle
always add up to 180°." As a contingent proposition, "Socrates was wise" might have
been false; that is, the state of affairs of Socrates' being wise might never have been
actualized. Since the truth value of "The angles of a triangle are 180°" is not dependent on any state of affairs' coming or failing to come into existence, there is no sense
at all in saying that it might have been false.

the laws governing that set, he could predict with complete certainty the events issuing from that set of causal conditions. If this could be done, it would certainly show a kind of necessity in history, and the knowledge of history would have a kind of certainty about it, though this necessity and this certainty would not be of the logical sort that Hegel perhaps believed in.

Climacus notes that even this causal necessity and causal certainty would not yield the kind of certainty that the rationalist mind pants after, because the necessity here is not an absolute necessity (as logical necessity is). As he says,

> Every cause ends in a freely acting cause. The intervening causes are mis-
> leading in that the coming into existence appears to be necessary; the truth
> about them is that they, as having themselves come into existence, *defini-*
> *tively* point back to a freely acting cause. As soon as coming into existence is
> definitively reflected upon, even an inference from natural law is not evi-
> dence of the necessity of any coming into existence. (75)

Climacus is saying something like this: Even if we ascribed causal necessity to everything inside nature (including human history), we would only have the necessity of this or that event *relative to* other events inside nature. If we think definitively about coming into existence, however, we will see that the change from nonbeing to existence is always a transition from possibil- ity to actuality, and possibility as such does not speak, as it were, in favor of one possibility over another. It is not as though we have some possibili- ties that are, simply as possibilities, more pregnant than others. As possi- bilities, all are equally actualizable. If we ask why some possibilities get actualized and others do not, we may be inclined to point to the causal grounds. This answer, Climacus is saying, is shortsighted and provisional. Even if we can explain the actualization of possibility a by reference to the actualizations of other possibilities (which are the causal antecedents for a) still this string of possibilities is only one among an indefinitely large set of strings. Even if we believe that there is no gratuitous fiddling with the string once it is initiated, still we can ask why this string, rather than any one of the others, got actualized. To address this question (as opposed to remain- ing silent), thinks Climacus, is to postulate some "freely acting cause," a cause that itself cannot be accounted for by reference to items in the string. If the postulated cause is not thus free (but instead a subsequent part of a string), then the question arises again, "Why this string?" Whereas if the postulated cause is free, the question is answered, however unsatisfying the answer may be to rationalists.

The answer is unsatisfactory to someone looking for Promethean cer- tainty in his historical judgments, because he would like to have them tied down without any loose ends at all. This answer leaves an enormous loose end at the beginning of things, even if, by some astounding state of human science, we grasped the contingent necessity (as we may now call it) of the events to be explained. Only logical necessity, not causal necessity, could satisfy the compulsion to tie down all the epistemic loose ends. Perhaps it is the insane courage of Hegel to have faced this fact head-on and tried unflinchingly to see logical necessity in the events of history. Climacus's Interlude is an effort to call the bluff that is surely at the bottom of such an ill-conceived enterprise.

God is the freely effecting cause to which Climacus says every causal chain ultimately points back. Even if everything that happens within the creation happens by causal necessity, still every event is non-necessary in the sense that God could have actualized other creations—other chains of events—than the one he did actualize. He could have done so because these other creations were possibilities, which is to say that although they did not in fact get actualized, there was no necessity that they did not. By the same token, the creation that is might not have been.

A possibility that Climacus seems not to consider is that God, though distinct from nature and bringing it into being, is not a freely effecting cause. Perhaps there is something about God's character that necessitates both that he make a nature and that he make precisely the one he did make. If so, then it would seem that the rationalist, by knowing not only all the facts and laws of nature, but also the ironclad laws of God's nature, could in principle know everything with the kind of certainty he is seeking. Climacus might respond in two ways.

First, he might say that a "first cause" that had the inner necessity we have mentioned would not sufficiently resemble what people have called God. Indeed, such a "god" would be just a pretemporal state of the universe, and not a creator of it, much less a person. Thus the suggestion reduces to a simple denial that the universe cannot be causally determined all the way down, and an openness to the possibility of atheism that, as we have seen, Climacus finds unthinkable.

More powerfully he might point out that even if we can conceive of something distinct from nature and history that is the cause of it, and yet "acts" by natural necessity, this will not help the rationalist to achieve the certainty of historical judgment that he desires. The difficulty with postulating a preuniverse necessity in hope of gaining certainty of judgment about the events of history is that the expedient offers no real hope. Certainty of judgment even in meteorology requires a large and detailed mastery, presently unattainable, of the facts of a given weather situation, as well as a perfect grasp of the principles that govern transition from one state of the weather to another. In meteorology we are at least dealing with facts and principles that are *in principle* accessible through inquiry. But it is hard even to imagine how one might go about learning the ironclad necessities that make up the nature of the prenature state of "god." They will certainly have to be learned if we are to have any hope of building certainty of knowledge on them. One can speculate that Hegel sought to fulfill his rationalist yearnings through the route of logic rather than of empirical science precisely because it takes little more than rational insight to gain certainty here, whereas gaining certainty through the mastery of causal connections is practically an endlessly detailed task. Hegel was after something more than the mere logical possibility of science.

So far, then, there is one agent in the universe who has options. For the sake of argument we have been assuming the thesis of determinism, which includes all human actions among the events of nature that are causally necessary. But Climacus distinguishes the coming into existence of natural occurrences from a coming into existence "in the stricter sense," and says, "The more special historical coming into existence comes into existence by way of a relatively freely acting cause" (76). Such a cause is, of course, a human being, a being who is able, by surveying his world, to see and choose among options in it. A human is, among the creatures of the earth, alone historical not just because he came into being, but because he is aware of his past, evaluates it, and carries it with him into the future. He comes to take responsibility for his past and becomes aware, with help from his knowledge of the past, of the options that the future holds. In short, he knows his history and through knowing it creates more of it. As Climacus says, he is "dialectical with respect to time" (76). By contrast, the rest of nature is *in* time but does not *grasp* time for itself. Here Climacus perhaps oversimplifies nature. He tends to think of all of nature on the model of such things as mountains, oak trees, and chickens, which do not learn much from the past and do not anticipate the future. The higher animals seem to be able to do these things to a limited extent. Dogs and chimpanzees learn from past experiences, and though they do not apprehend as many options of action or possess as many means of effecting their choices as humans do, they are certainly not as blind to past and future as potatoes.

But these capacities are not enough to render the higher animals historical in the strictest sense. For "coming into existence can contain within itself a redoubling, that is, a possibility of a coming into existence within its own coming into existence" (76). Here Climacus seems to be referring (I admit obscurely) to the human potential for becoming a self. To become a self is not just to generate an awareness of options with respect to the future by the help of past experiences, but to generate an awareness of a compelling option with respect to something outside the "temporal" boundaries of one's own life, with the help of a synoptic assessment of one's entire life within those boundaries. To become a self is to despair over the realm of the "temporal" or "finite." Since one can choose to refuse to acknowledge one's need for God, becoming a self is a matter of freedom, just as the choice between any other two genuine options is a matter of freedom. It is "historical" because seeing the option of a God-relationship at all is grounded in the human capacity to survey one's past and future—the same capacity that grounds the freedom with which one chooses options within time.

Climacus's present point, however, is merely that people have genuine options just as God has, though they have far fewer than he, and have what options they possess only at his sufferance. Climacus does not argue that humans have freedom. He asserts it dogmatically, as a belief highly congruent with and perhaps even necessarily implied by Christianity, and seemingly also implied by ordinary moral conceptions, such as guilt and responsibility. People's having options entails an obvious unhappy consequence for anyone who hopes to achieve a deductive certainty of historical truths. For if humans have options, then they are likely to be interfering constantly in the causal nexus in such a way that the causal laws from which, along with certain facts, one attempts to deduce the historical truths, will not always be operative. Indeed, in the normal sense of "historical event," all historical events would be infected with this sort of indeterminacy.

Thus, that some events can in principle be deduced from facts and causal laws does not imply the possibility of knowing historical truths with the kind of certainty that a rationalist may hope for. Even assuming the truth of determinism, historical events are necessary only relatively to other events, since the entire system of actual events is only one possibility among many. But if determinism is false and there are agents acting in history who have genuine options, then no historical events consequent upon actions taken by such agents can be known even with the more modest certainty that can hold for truths deducible from causal laws.

HISTORICAL BELIEFS
AND "IMMEDIATE COGNITION"

So far the Interlude seems to be on solid ground. The exposition may be excessively obscure, the position refuted may sometimes appear too weak to warrant such an expenditure of effort and, as Climacus warned us (72-73), he may repeat himself a lot; but when the arguments are ferreted out it appears that he is on the right track. The kind of certainty the rationalist is after cannot be had in the realm of historical facts, by ascribing either logical or causal necessity to such facts.

In the second half of the Interlude Climacus considers a third possible way that historical knowledge might be absolutely certain, namely, by "immediate sensation and immediate cognition," which, as he admits, "cannot deceive." The grasping of historical events does include an "immediate" element. But this is not enough to make any historical beliefs certain, because of another factor in them, namely, that the event in question has come into existence, and this, he says, "cannot be sensed immediately" (81). It is upon these observations that Climacus builds his positive account of historical judgment.

Essentially, "the organ for the historical" (81) is belief. One of the contexts in which we say we believe something (for example, "I believe that so-and-so is by far the best of the presidential candidates") is that in which we acknowledge a certain objective dubiousness about our claim, and so would hesitate to say we know, and yet express solid commitment to it, even certainty about it. Historical claims all have this logical structure, according to Climacus: they are based on an immediate deliverance to the senses, but something that is not (and cannot be) thus delivered to the senses is affirmed about what is thus delivered. This nonimmediate something is coming-into-existence, and this is affirmed with certainty in the face of objective uncertainty.

> Faith believes what it does not see; it does not believe that the star is there, for that it sees, but it believes that the star has come into existence. The same holds true of an event. The occurrence can be known immediately but not that it has occurred, not even that it is in the process of occurring, even though it is taking place, as they say, right in front of one's nose. (81-82)

It might seem, says Climacus, that the objective uncertainty as to whether something immediately apprehended has come into existence is overcome by inferring that since what is apprehended is an effect, it must have a cause, and thus must have come into existence. This would be a mistake since the judgment that what is in front of our noses is an effect is itself a matter of belief, and so is subject to the same uncertainty as coming into existence. So historical belief is not an inference, but "an act of will" (82), "a resolution" (84) to take what is immediately presented as having come into existence. Thus "belief is not a knowledge, but an act of freedom, an expression of will" (83). There is, it seems, no such thing as historical knowledge, but only passionate affirmations (see 84) of historical claims. So much for those who themselves witness the events about which they make historical claims; what about those who affirm historical claims on the basis of testimony? Their case is exactly analogous to the basic case outlined above.

> Instead of having the immediacy of sensation and cognition (which, however, cannot apprehend the historical), the person who is not contemporary with the historical has the report of contemporaries, to which he relates in the same manner as the contemporaries to the immediacy. . . . The one who comes later does indeed believe by virtue of the contemporary's declaration, but only in the same sense as the contemporary believes by virtue of immediate sensation and cognition. (85)

What shall we make of this theory? We can assess it only by getting clearer about some of its main terms, "immediate," "coming into existence," and "uncertainty."

What does Climacus mean by "immediate"? What first strikes the reader about this term is that it seems to express for him two different, and inconsistent, concepts. On the one hand he says that immediate sensation cannot deceive, and speaks approvingly of traditional skeptics who succeed in avoiding any dubious epistemic commitments by refusing to commit themselves to anything beyond the immediate. This might lead us to suppose that by "immediate sensation" he means an experience insofar as it is noncommittal with respect to objects (objects being what the experience is "about"). Let us call such an experience an "object-noncommittal sense presentation." If there were such things as object-noncommittal sense presentations, and they could somehow be picked out, then sincere reports of them would perhaps be incapable of being in error. However, only a little reflection will show that the hope of getting at an immediate experience in this sense is vain.

I am in the Rocky Mountains sitting by a stream watching the water rush over the rocks. If I have recently been reading science textbooks, I may construe the scene before me thus: "That is liquid H_2O being drawn by gravity over granite surfaces." This will not count as an immediate sensation in any philosopher's book. For whatever sense-experiences I am having here are mediated by some object-concepts of chemistry and physics that are by no means delivered "in" the sense-experiences. To get to the immediate sensation I will have to withdraw such conceptual schemes as this, seeing just what is right there in the experience, so to speak. What is immediately and obviously before me, then? The first answer that occurs to me is that I see water flowing over rocks. With a moment's reflection I realize that concepts like water and flowing and rocks are in their own way as richly articulated and associated with matters not immediately before me as are the concepts of hydrogen and gravity. So whatever I am having an immediate sense-experience of is not water flowing over rocks, either. So I try to reduce out the rock-relativity, water-relativity, and so forth, of my experience, and just examine the experience itself. I try to see my experience in terms of patches of light and dark, texture, shape, and so forth. I see that I must distinguish light-patches that have a sparkly character from those that have a flatter character, that there are various complications and grades in between, and so forth. But now I realize that this way of having my experience is parasitic upon the object concepts that I was trying to get away from. For to speak of "patches," "texture," "shape," "sparkly," "flat"—even to think in terms of colors and light and dark—is to borrow concepts from the fund that also includes rocks and water and flowing. Perhaps over long usage of these concepts in their new, sense-presentation context, the metaphoric dependence on object concepts could be killed, and I could get a set of pure sense-presentation concepts in terms of which to construe my experience. But, "*Concepts* in terms of which to *construe*"? That was just what I was trying to escape from, for I was trying to experience just what was in the presentations of sense *by themselves* ("immediately"). So it turns out that my experience is just as non-"immediate" after I have gone to all the trouble to develop this extremely sophisticated and unnatural way to think of my experiences as it was before. Indeed, construing my experiences as mere sense presentations, even if it is possible, is in one sense far less immediate than just relaxing and seeing water flowing over rocks, or even H_2O being pulled by gravity over granite. It is less immediate in that it is more difficult, sophisticated, fancy, and unnatural. One might even suspect that, like other fancy and unnatural ways of apprehending things, this one would be more subject to error than everyday garden-variety seeing.

As I said, it is not clear that Climacus is committed to this sense of "immediate" anyway. Our reason for suspecting that he is not is the examples he chooses of things that can be known immediately. He says that faith "does not believe that the star exists, for that it sees, but it believes that the star has come into existence" (81). If seeing the star is an example of immediate knowledge, then clearly he does not mean by "immediate sensation" "object-noncommittal sense presentation." To see a star is to make use of the concept of star, a concept that is different from others that might be used, such as planet or satellite or hole in the canopy. This fact, however, has the consequence that seeing a star is not immune from error in the way Climacus says immediate sensation is. One can think one sees a star when in fact one is seeing a planet.

The same goes for Climacus's comment about a person's stance towards historical testimony. He says that we stand to a piece of historical testimony "in the same manner as the contemporaries [stand] to the immediacy" (85). Clearly we do not apprehend the words of historical testimony in the way we would apprehend object-noncommittal sense presentations. We apprehend them as words of a particular language, with a sense that may be ambiguous as between two conflicting interpretations, which may require sophisticated knowledge to understand, and so forth. Thus again, a person can think he understands a piece of historical testimony and be wrong. If this is immediate sensation or cognition, then clearly it is not immune from error.

What shall we say, then? Does Climacus mean 'immediate sensation' in the manner suggested by the skeptics, or in the more ordinary manner, according to which we can immediately perceive stars, understand reports, and so forth? I think we can safely say that it does not matter, for the theory is in trouble either way. If we interpret it in the first way, then immediate sensation is something that none of us ever experience, and possibly never could experience under even the most ideal conditions. If we interpret "immediate sensation" in the second manner, then while it is obvious that we have experiences of immediate sensation, it is equally obvious that they are not immune from error. I think it is worth wondering whether by this rather blatant inconsistency in the use of one of the key terms of his theory, Climacus is not gently prodding us, like a Socrates, to give birth to better ideas ourselves. I shall not be dogmatic on the point, nor need I be. For the result will be the same regardless of what Johannes Climacus intended.

Let us now take a look at Climacus's use of the concept of coming-into-existence, and his claim that this cannot be an object of immediate knowledge. First, we must distinguish two senses of "come into existence," one commonsensical and the other philosophical. It is the philosophical sense upon which his theory trades, but his example of the star may mislead the reader into understanding him more commonsensically. He says that we can immediately see that the star exists, but can only believe that it came into existence. Here to say the star came into existence is to point to that time or time period in which an event or series of events occurred that is the origination of the star. Since a person who views a star (almost?) never also views this event of origination, it makes common sense to say that nobody ever perceives the coming into existence of a star, but at most believes that it did one time come into existence. Analogous events of origination would be the conception of a baby, the building of a new gymnasium, the formation of a new government. We look at a cornfield one autumn, and then through the winter we see certain events taking place: the digging of foundations, the laying of bricks, the stringing of wires, and so forth. Then in the spring there stands on the former cornfield a new gymnasium. Through a series of events, all witnessable, the gym has come into existence. This kind of coming into existence we might designate "momentous initiation." It is the initiation into existence of something momentous enough to us that we pick it out from other things, attribute identity through time to it, and take an interest in its point of origin.

Climacus's theory is not limited to momentous initiations, as common sense would tend to be when it talks about things coming into existence. Climacus intends his theory to be applicable to any state of affairs whatsoever. Every actualization of a possibility is, in this philosophical sense, a coming into existence. Thus, the state of affairs of the 14,659th brick of the gym being in place can come into existence, even though in common sense nobody would be likely to pick this one out from among the millions of others like it that might be picked out.

Maybe our example is poor, since it seems implausible that someone could know by immediate sensation that the 14,659th brick is in place—not just if we interpret "immediate sensation" to mean "object-noncommittal sense-presentation," but even if we interpret it commonsensically. One would seem to have to do a lot of counting or record-keeping to know that this state of affairs exists; it could not be grasped just by looking, normally. (In this, we might note by the way, this state of affairs is very much like most historical events. It is not only impossible by "immediate sensation" to tell whether something has come into existence; it is even impossible to tell, without considerable reflection and auxiliary knowledge, what state of affairs is before us.) So, let us take another example that is not subject to this complexity, one which can be said to happen "right in front of one's nose" (82).

I am sitting on the bank of that Rocky Mountain stream contemplating the currents when I see, dancing on the riffles upstream, an aspen leaf. As it arrives at the rocks a short distance from me it catches on one of them and sticks there for a second or two. According to Climacus, I can immediately apprehend that the state of affairs of the aspen leaf catching on the rock exists (or existed); but I must believe that it came into existence. What about this? It makes sense to say that I cannot immediately apprehend the coming into existence of the star, since its coming into existence occurred long before my birth. But I saw the rock and leaf before the event, and then I saw the leaf catch. This seems a clear case of seeing a state of affairs come into existence. It would be outlandish, if this happens in front of my nose, to say that I saw that the aspen leaf caught on the rock, but can only believe that this state of affairs came into existence. Indeed, the kind of doubt of which this state of affairs is susceptible is not as to whether it came into existence, but as to whether the state of affairs that I think came into existence is the one that did. If called to task I am likely to say, "Well, it might have been a birch-leaf rather than aspen, or maybe it was even a bubble-gum wrapper; and perhaps what I took for a rock was really a log; but whether this state of affairs, which I admit I may have misperceived, came into existence, is as far beyond doubt as anything I know of."

Of course, in speaking this way I am assuming a roughly commonsensical interpretation of "immediate cognition"—roughly, that is, what the common person means when he says, "I saw it with my own eyes." Here knowing by direct perception would be in contrast with knowing something by inference, or on authority, by hearsay, or by some interpretation. Suppose we interpret "immediate cognition" in the other way suggested by Climacus's text? Perhaps it means "object-noncommittal sense presentation." Admittedly, even if there were an immediate sensation of a state of affairs in this sense, there would still probably be no such thing as an immediate sensation of the coming into existence of that state of affairs, since there seems to be something like an object commitment in the assertion that something has come into existence. But to use this expedient for excluding coming into existence from among the things that can be known immediately is like burning the house down to get rid of the cockroaches. To limit immediate cognition to object-noncommittal sense presentations is to admit that *nothing at all* that counts as humanly significant data—that such-and-such is a star, an aspen leaf, a rock, water, that so-and-so said something, and so forth—can be known immediately and with certainty. I conclude that if there is any humanly significant knowledge that can be treated as immediate, direct, and certain, coming into existence is in this domain.

The supposition that we can know by immediate cognition that a star exists, and yet not know whether it has come into existence, also seems to be defeated by something Climacus says earlier. He begins the Interlude by speaking of three categories, the necessary, the possible, and the actual. The latter two belong together: the possible is the possibly actual, and the actual is the actualization of what is possible. "Necessity," by contrast, "stands all by itself" (74). The realm of the necessary is not a realm of possibilities, and nothing that is actual is necessary, but instead is only actualized possibility. The difficulty in Climacus's theory is exposed if we ask to which of these three categories belongs what I know when I know that a star exists. Climacus certainly does not want to admit that the star may exist necessarily, but neither is it a mere possibility. So it seems that the star is an actuality. But an actuality must be an actualized possibility. But what is an actualized possibility, if not a possibility that has come into existence? Thus, if I can know by immediate cognition that something is actual, I cannot doubt, except by a confusion of categories, that it has come into existence. The only way to doubt whether something that is actual has come into existence is to suppose that it may be necessary. But that would be to forget Climacus's grammatical remark that necessity stands all by itself.

There is one more fairly large hole in Climacus's theory of historical judgments that we must notice before we start looking through these holes at some historical judgments, and so try to learn from him as from a Socratic teacher. The elements of Climacus's theory that I have so far examined are not peculiar to a theory of historical judgments, except in the broad sense in which any nongeneral empirical judgment, being about something that happens in time, is historical. But his theory is also about historical judgments in the more ordinary sense of judgments about the past, and in particular judgments we must base on other people's testimonies. When we make a historical judgment based on some testimony, we stand related to the testimony in the same manner, avers Climacus, as we would have stood to the deliverances of immediate sense and cognition if we had been present with our eyes and noses at the occurrence of the reported event.

Let us say that one afternoon I peer out my kitchen window and see a Mercedes drive through a four-way stop, colliding into the left side of a Chevrolet that has proceeded to cross the intersection. The Mercedes then backs up and drives away. According to one interpretation of "immediate," Climacus holds that I perceive this much by immediate cognition. Then I call the police and make a report of the occurrence. Will the sergeant stand in the same relation to my report as I stand to my immediate cognition? If Climacus is right that I believe, but do not know, that something has happened that has happened before my very eyes, I can surely at least say that my belief is very near at hand. Maybe I can doubt my eyes, but normally it would not be natural for me to do so. If I know myself to be subject to hallucinations, or suspect that the "accident" is a scene from a movie being filmed in my neighborhood, I may have some genuine doubts about what I "see"; but in normal circumstances the "belief" that the accident happened follows so naturally upon seeing it happen as to be unquestionable. Indeed, under normal circumstances it seems misleading to say that I only believe that the accident happened, but do not know it.

Does the sergeant stand in the same relation to my testimony as I stand to my eyes? Obviously not; my testimony does not naturally beget, in the sergeant's mind, the same full readiness to affirm that this accident came into existence, that my immediate experience begets in me. Many doubts are reasonable for him that are not reasonable for me. For all he knows, I may be a crank interested in annoying the police department, or a hysteric who saw an accident, but misdescribed it as a hit-and-run. Or maybe I am not very knowledgeable about cars, and really saw a Ford Granada rather than a Mercedes. Or maybe the sergeant is aware of the movie that is being filmed in my neighborhood, and wonders on that basis whether what I saw was a real accident, and so forth.

Of course, if the sergeant takes the trouble to interrogate me, skillfully eliminating by his questions such possibilities of error one by one, my testimony can be upgraded as a basis for his believing that the accident I report has happened. Indeed, my testimony under such rigorous elicitation may in the end prove a worthier ground for his belief than my immediate cognition is for my own. But the fact that testimony can be so upgraded is no basis for saying that testimony as such is on all fours with immediate cognition.

To generalize: Historical testimony is subject to dubiety in many ways that immediate experiences are not. If one has a historical document that claims the occurrence of certain events, one may wonder (1) what the claims mean, that is, what events are being claimed here to have occurred; (2) whether, assuming it is clear what is being claimed, the document is genuine rather than a hoax; (3) whether, assuming the document genuine, the witness can be relied upon to be giving an accurate account: that is, (a) whether he is not lying about what he saw or heard; (b) whether he was not an innocent victim of delusion or mistake; (c) whether he did not see the event through an interpretive scheme that the reader of the account might consider primitive, distorting or otherwise inadequate; and (4) whether, assuming the writer a reliable witness, the document has not been subsequently tampered with. When a historian reads a "source," such questions as these are very often reasonable ones to ask; but analogies of these doubts are either nonexistent or comparatively rare for the person who witnesses the event itself.

I blush to write down these truisms. It is perhaps salutary to make them explicit, to enforce upon the reader's mind the impression that Climacus's theory of historical judgments is maybe presented tongue in cheek—an impression that Climacus's abstruse style may serve to mitigate. Our discussion has brought to light four implausibilities gross enough to arouse in us a modest suspicion that Climacus would have us rethink his statements for ourselves.

First is the matter of immediate sensation. It would be too much to expect Climacus to be acquainted with twentieth-century philosophy of perception. But not only does part of his account seem subject to correction from that quarter; it is obviously at odds with itself. For he says that immediate cognition cannot deceive and within the same paragraph offers as an example of such cognition the judgment "what I am seeing is a star which exists," a judgment clearly capable of being wrong.

Second, while it is beyond doubt that there are many objective uncertainties attaching to historical judgments, it seems ludicrous to focus on coming into existence as a special locus of objective uncertainty. If, of Climacus's two competing uses of 'immediate cognition', we accept the more commonsensical one, there seems to be no reason to deny that we have immediate cognitions of coming into existence.

Third, he seems to contradict himself in claiming that we can immediately perceive that an event exists and yet doubt whether it has come into existence. For events would seem to be actualities, and actualities are actualized possibilities, and actualization of possibilities is just what coming into existence, in the philosophical sense of the phrase, is. Consequently, it follows from something's existence being given to immediate cognition that it has come into existence.

Fourth, it is hard to believe that Climacus means seriously that recipients of historical testimony stand related to the testimony in the same manner as they would have stood to what they would have seen with their eyes, had they been witnesses of the testified event.

SUBJECTIVITY AND CERTAINTY
IN HISTORICAL JUDGMENTS

If we strike out the implausibilities in Climacus's theory, is there anything left? I think so. Our reinterpretation will take the form of relativizing the notion of immediate cognition and broadening the concept of belief. While denying the existence of absolutely immediate cognitions, we must accord legitimacy, indeed a foundational status, to what someone (myself or someone else) "sees with his eyes and hears with his ears." Such experiences are where our claims about history begin, however far beyond them we may eventually travel.

We deny Climacus's claim that the subjective certainty of historical judgments is achieved, one judgment at a time, by a willful act of affirming the coming-into-existence of the corresponding fact. But we have to admit there is a subjective element at the foundation of such judgments and that this is fittingly summarized as "belief." In the course of the discussion it will become evident that historical judgments are founded in different ways upon beliefs, and upon different kinds of beliefs.

Some beliefs we might call *methodological.* These are beliefs without which we could not get historical reasoning going at all. They are analogous to the machinist's belief in his calipers, without which he could not begin with the business of machining. An example would be the belief that a report of what a man has done on one occasion is capable of corroborating the claim that he has done something similar on another occasion. A second kind of belief can be called *factual.* Thus, my belief that the Chevrolet continued down the street, rather than stopping half a block away, is part of the foundation for my judgment that what I saw out my kitchen window was a hit-and-run. A third kind of belief can be called *sensitizing.* Such beliefs are evaluative; they are about what is important and what is unimportant, and they have the effect of determining emphasis and grounding insight in historical accounts. An example, which I will discuss in a few pages, is the moral belief that all persons ought to be accorded dignity. It is beliefs of these three kinds (and, for all I know, others as well) that supply the womb in which immediate cognitions grow into historical judgments.

Historical judgments must claim a foundation in "immediate cognition," not in the incoherent mode of object-noncommittal sense presentations, but in the commonsensical mode. That is, they must purport to be a simple report of a cognition (something seen, heard, and so forth) by an "eyewitness," or to be a construal of such a cognition under terms of some interpretive framework, or to be a construal of immediate cognitions not had by the maker of the judgment but traceable via some record to the cognitions of such an "eyewitness." Judgments of real historical interest, however, are never just more or less atomistic reports of data; they always go beyond immediate cognition, even immediate cognition thought of in this nonphilosophical sense. Historical facts are not brutes, at least not utterly; they are always more or less civilized, domesticated animals, cultivated, proliferated, groomed and fenced in by their human masters and caretakers. They are always *constructions* upon the data provided by the merest seeing and hearing. Historical judgments are the orientation for and the consequences of stories, that is, construals of the data by virtue of some ordering of them. This constructive character of historical judgments corresponds to Climacus's claim that there is always an element of "belief" in them.

Consequently historical judgments are always "objectively uncertain" in the sense that there are other constructions that might conceivably be put upon the same data. As Climacus notes, the objective uncertainty does not imply, either factually or normatively, a subjective one; for even if you reflect on some alternative and incompatible ways of constructing the data, you may not find any of them appealing. Provided that your epistemic metabolism has not run amuck through association with rationalist philosophers, you will not begin to doubt until some alternative and incompatible construction begins to enter into serious competition with your judgment.

The difference between Climacus and my reinterpretation of him is that he seems to think that "belief" is an act of will that a person performs when confronted with an experience or a testimony; whereas I will hold that the confidence of the individual in affirming the historical judgment—the lack of any doubt on his part—is a consequence of that judgment's fitting together into a pattern with other judgments he and his community are willing to make, and of its fitting together too with patterns of behavior and insight that he has found to be workable, and that have thus become a confirmed part of his character.

Just as the machinist's trust of his calipers is basic for all sorts of daily judgments he makes about how big things are and what will fit into what, every historical judgment depends on other historical judgments that the historian just does not question. Just as a moral man's belief in the rights of the individual is foundational for all sorts of other judgments that he makes about the rightness of individual actions and institutions, our historical judgments are founded on beliefs about what constitutes reliability in a record or a witness, about what is a plausible candidate for having happened, about what are acceptable patterns of inference from data, and so forth. When a particular judgment "fits" with other beliefs that are firmly in place for us, and that can thus function as foundations, then that judgment gains certainty for us. The point to notice is that there is no absolute foundation—no foundation that is eternally exempt from questioning and uncertainty; there are only foundations that are in fact, in the long run of a human practice, not questioned. It is not, as Climacus seems to think, that we perform an act of believing for each historical judgment we make, which certifies it. Rather, the certainty with which a particular judgment is made derives from its being supported in a web of beliefs, of life-vindicated commitments.

While this view does not preserve the letter of Climacus's theory it does, it seems to me, preserve the spirit of it. For what he wants above all to affirm is that there is a personal or subjective ingredient in historical judgments, that this ingredient is a legitimate, nay inescapable facet of them and that such judgments are properly certified (that is, rendered certain and legitimate) in part by this subjective facet.

Now I think we are in a position to appreciate Climacus's strange claim that I bear the same relation to a testimony as I would have borne to the deliverances of immediate cognition, had I been an eyewitness of the event that is the subject of the testimony. He claims that in both cases the certainty with which I make the historical judgment is a function of "belief." On my rethinking, that claim would amount to this: In both cases the certainty or lack thereof with which I make the judgment is largely determined by the way the proposed judgment fits or fails to fit with other beliefs that function, for me, as possible foundations of the judgment in question. As I noted in my criticism of Climacus's formulation, there are a number of needed beliefs that may easily fail to be in place in connection with testimonies, most of which are irrelevant for an eyewitness: what the testimony means, whether the document in which it is lodged is genuine, whether the witnesses whose testimony is preserved are trustworthy, whether the document is in a sufficiently original condition to be reliable, and so forth. So the kind of beliefs that must be in place for me, if I am to accept with certainty an ordinary historical claim based on testimony, may differ from the kind that support the judgment of an eyewitness. But a claim based on one's own seeing and hearing is also based on beliefs. Let us look first at a case of a historical judgment based on testimony.

If we judge from the Gospel of Mark that Jesus of Nazareth claimed the authority of God for himself, one could conceivably raise these doubts: What does it mean to claim the authority of God? Is this something that people in Jesus' day did as a matter of course, perhaps with tongue in cheek as a kind of theological joke? Or are the supposed claims maybe just a minor variation on what the prophets regularly did, and not at all a claim to be equal with God? And what about the document itself? We know that there have been literary hoaxes such as the Donation of Constantine, an eighth-century document claiming to be the work of the Emperor Constantine, and very useful for bolstering the authority of the bishops of Rome. Might not Mark be a similar hoax? But assuming that Mark is of ancient origin, composed on the basis of documents originally made by eyewitnesses or interviewers of eyewitnesses, are these eyewitnesses and interviewers trustworthy? Is it not plausible that they were uncritical and impressionable people, and that because of Jesus' extraordinary personal magnetism, or for some reason unknowable by us, they began to ascribe to him an authoritative demeanor and mode of speech not his own? Once these critical questions are raised, the rational believer that Jesus claimed the authority of God will have to believe also that it is plausible to interpret words and actions ascribed to Jesus in Mark as claims of divine authority, that Mark is an ancient document, that the witnesses to whom the document is ultimately indebted are in general sober-minded, not given to flights of fancy and gratuitous invention. Any serious inability to affirm these things (or things like them) will entrain the inability to affirm that Jesus claimed to have divine authority.

Now let us turn to the case of the eyewitness. I shall imagine that you are such a person, one who has an "immediate cognition," as Climacus calls it, of Jesus' claiming to be God. Let us say that you are one of the scribes standing by when Jesus says to the paralytic, "My son, your sins are forgiven." I shall interview you, to bring out the way in which your judgment is founded upon beliefs. You say, "This is blasphemy; who can forgive sins but God alone?"

> I: But did you hear him right? You will have to admit that sometimes we miss a word or two, and the proposition we hear turns out to be different from the proposition that was uttered. The crowd was making a bit of a rumble in the background, after all.
>
> You: I heard him clearly enough.
>
> I: Okay. So we have one belief operating so far. You believe he made a blasphemous claim, and when I question you, it shows that behind this belief was the belief that you heard him clearly. Now, how do you know you heard him clearly?
>
> You: I am thirty-four years old, and have considerable experience of hearing clearly and hearing poorly, and I believe that I can distinguish the two.
>
> I: Good. So we have isolated two of your background beliefs. Here is another question: How do you know that in speaking these words he does not really mean just to say that *God* forgives this wretch's sins? After all, the Bible you are so adept at interpreting speaks in many places of God's willingness to forgive sinners. *Must* you interpret him as pronouncing his own forgiveness of the paralytic?
>
> You: Well, you could tell from the authoritative tone of voice that this blasphemy is what he meant.
>
> I: But is not the perception of an "authoritative tone of voice" an awfully subjective matter? Did everyone hear it that way? And if they did, what would that prove?
>
> You: If my judgment about the matter does not satisfy you, let me tell you this: My fellow scribes and I have had our eye on this fellow for sev-

eral weeks now, because we got wind that this was a *pattern* with him. The way he uses "my Father" in reference to the Holy One of Israel, and the way he pronounces the Law, are all in the same pattern. There is no doubt what he means by this forgiving of sins.

I: Now I am beginning to get the picture. You were not an eyewitness of all the different ways this man commits blasphemy. Some of it you trust others for, and then you interpret what you see in light of what you have heard. Our belief-count seems to be up to four. But tell me, how do you know that the others are telling the truth?

You: Of course, I cannot be absolutely sure they have not exaggerated or distorted one tale or another. This fellow puts them off, no doubt, and I am willing to admit they may not be completely objective about him. But in general I am perfectly satisfied with the thrust of their testimony. It forms a consistent pattern on the whole, and further it accords very nicely with what I have seen myself.

I: Let me see if I understand you. You seem to be saying that you trust some of the things your friends say because they fit with other things they say. And you trust your interpretation of what you have seen with your own eyes, partly because of what you have heard from others; and you trust what you hear from others because it is supported by your interpretation of what you see? In general, you seem to believe that a report of what a man does on one occasion is capable of lending some corroboration to the claim that he has done something similar on another, separate occasion?

You: That is correct. Are those not ways we come to many judgments and, I might add, successfully and happily? Would not my powers of judgment, even as an eyewitness, be utterly paralyzed, if I did not trust patterns of thinking such as these?

The answer, of course, is yes. I do not mean for a moment to doubt the veracity and objectivity of the scribe's eyewitness report, but only to point out how it—and by implication any historical judgment whatsoever—is grounded in beliefs that in principle might be called into question. Most of them are not in fact called into question, and so no serious doubts arise with respect to them. Philosophical skeptics are people who notice that our claims of knowledge rest on foundations that can be imagined to be false, and then go on fallaciously to conclude that the foundations are in fact unsteady.

The noncontemporary does not, therefore, bear the same relation to testimony as the eyewitness bears to his own immediate experience. Yet the judgments to which each comes on the basis of his "data" have this in common: In each case the judgment gets its certification by its relation to other beliefs that, for the moment, play the role of foundations. (I say "for the moment" because many of these beliefs can in turn be questioned; and then still others may be appealed to as their foundations. Some of what I have called "methodological" and "sensitizing" beliefs may not be groundable in other beliefs. If they are questioned, the appropriate response is to point to the loss in quality of our human life, or even the impossibility of carrying it on at all, which would result from their abandonment.) It is because historical judgments are thus systemic or relational, certified by other beliefs, that some judgments that have no basis at all in our immediate cognition are more firmly grounded and certain for us than some that are based on what we have seen with our own eyes. Thus, it is considerably more certain that there lived a man named Thomas Jefferson who had a great influence on early American politics, than it is that what I saw five minutes ago through my kitchen window was a hit-and-run automobile accident. The reason is that the structure of beliefs that supports the former judgment is much greater and more solid than the structure that supports my eyewitness judgment.

ON RECOGNIZING JESUS

So much for historical judgments in general. Perhaps we can get clearer about the force of Climacus's theory by orienting and then narrowing our field of vision. Let us begin with a rough and broad distinction between two kinds of historical questions, "find-out" and "judgment" questions. Of course, answers to historical questions are all judgments in the broad philosophical sense of the word. But they do not all require the complex mental background required by some questions, as when we say, "That's a matter of judgment," and call in people whose qualifications include some special web of beliefs, rare and difficult to acquire. Find-out questions are ones such as "Who killed Martin Luther King?" and "What books did Søren Kierkegaard read from on 5 May 1840?" Answering them may require considerable sleuthing, and in the end may be possible only in terms of a certain probability or not at all. But the answer to such questions presents no problem of understanding. Once the answer has been found, it can be communicated without further trouble by naming the killer, by naming the volumes. And it is in principle possible that the answer could be discovered in a similarly simple fashion—by an eyewitness of the murder, by finding a note in Kierkegaard's diary.

Second, there are many different sorts of historical judgment of the "judgment" type, and one of the ways they differ is according to subject matter. There are questions about institutions, battles, political movements, ideas, societies, and individual people. Answering them, and understanding the answers to them, requires a background of beliefs about the entity under consideration. Answers to "What caused the Great Depression?" will hang in a web of economic beliefs that not just any person on the street will have available to him. If the question is, "Why was the battle of Austerlitz won by Napoleon and lost by the Austrians and the Prussians?" some of the beliefs in the web will have to be relatively technical ones of military science. If the question is "To what extent were the authors and sources for the Gospels uncritical and impressionable people, given to wishful thinking and flights of fancy?" the "judgment" required may be a power of psychological insight that can be aided, but by no means guaranteed, by a broad and deep scholarly reading of the Gospels and other ancient literature. If the question is, "What relation did Samuel Johnson's social conservatism bear to his attitude towards poor and powerless people?" it may be that an adequate construction of Johnson's mind on this matter will require a psychological insight that we can only call moral—indeed a kind of wisdom; the web of beliefs that constitute such wisdom are not the results of technical expertise as are those of economics and military science, but are developed by the ordinary living of an intelligent moral life. Such intelligence, while being "ordinary" in the sense of not requiring any technical training, is perhaps no less rare than expertise in economics and military science.

Climacus sandwiches his theory of historical judgments in between two chapters whose function is to delineate the grammar of "faith"—that is, the historical judgment that the man Jesus, from Nazareth, is the son of God and lamb of God. So the question to which this judgment might be considered an answer is, as historical questions go, one belonging to the category of biography. That is, it is the same type of question that we ask with the words, "What sort of person was so-and-so?" There are obvious problems associated with the word "sort" in Jesus' case. Indeed, Climacus is right in insisting on the stark discontinuity between the logic of inquiry into a person's personality traits (a perfectly legitimate historical activity) and "inquiry" as to whether Jesus is the son of God and redeemer. Nevertheless, if an inquiry into the nature of ordinary historical judgments is to throw any light at all on the grammar of faith, we are bound to learn more from examining a kind of historical judgment that is as much like the Christian one as we can find.

In his fine book *Samuel Johnson,* John Wain attempts to correct, or at least balance, an aspect of the picture of Johnson sketched by James Boswell, which has led to a standard judgment on Johnson's character.

> Johnson is a typical arch-conservative, someone who in the eternal tug of war between labour and capital tends to find that his sympathies are with capital; who wants social change to be either gradual and cautious, or not to happen at all; who favours existing institutions rather than radical new solutions.

Wain comments:

> This cap fits Johnson to some extent, but it obscures many of the finer and more humane points of his thinking: his opposition to colonialism and to every form of exploitation; his hatred of the slave trade; his pleas for a more mer-

ciful penal system; his insistence that the real test of any civilization lies in its treatment of the poor.[5]

What interests us here is that Boswell, who was so close to Johnson, could fail to see, or to see clearly, or at a minimum to cause others to see clearly, this humane or "liberal" aspect of Johnson's character. The data upon which Wain draws for his adjusted construction of Johnson were not unknown to Boswell; we can find references to many of them in Boswell's biography. Yet somehow, through the manner of Boswell's presentation and the points on which he elects to lay stress, there emerges a different, and perhaps less just, impression of Johnson's mind. If it is not a difference of data that grounds the two conceptions of Johnson, is it not the background of beliefs or commitments in which the two men "process" their data, that makes the difference? Perhaps it is something as simple as Wain's belief that it is important to be concerned for the oppressed and suffering and dispossessed, that causes him to give the data in his possession the weight he gives them. Wain, at any rate, gives a psychological interpretation of Boswell's obtuseness:

> Boswell was a sentimental-romantic Tory of a very different stripe. . . . being the son of a laird and a bit of a snob, he deferred to titled people, where Johnson, for all his support of "subordination," was just as likely to growl at them . . . being untroubled by any notion of the basic rights of the human being, he thought the slave trade an excellent institution. Boswell naturally highlights those moods and opinions of Johnson's that match his own. What we lose in his portrait is the deeply humanitarian Johnson, the man who from first to last rooted his life among the poor and outcast.[6]

In explaining Boswell's blind spot by reference to the state of his subjectivity, Wain is not suggesting that a person would write a better sketch of Johnson if he had no subjectivity at all, no definite opinions about what is important and what is not, by which to sort the data. A biographer has to sort the data in one way or another. The real question is, "Which sorting principles are more appropriate to the man under consideration?" Since beliefs that allow sorting of the details of Johnson's life are (some of them) more strictly personality traits than the beliefs, say, that would allow for formulating an explanation of the Great Depression, the question "Which sorting principles?" may amount in practice to the question, "Which kind of personality makes the better biographer of a man like Johnson?" Boswell was no doubt a brilliant biographer in many ways, and Wain does not deny it, but a still better biographer can be imagined. Boswell's deficiency might be put this way: In an important respect he was not morally qualified to appre-

---

[5]John Wain, *Samuel Johnson* (New York: The Viking Press, 1974) 13-14.
[6]Ibid.

ciate Johnson; what was needed was, in part, a man more like Johnson him-self.

One difference between the function of Wain's moral belief in grounding a more just portrait of Johnson, and the function of a typical grounding be-lief in the mind of an economist explaining the Great Depression, is that the economist can probably legitimately appeal to his belief in support of his explanation (in the expectation that other economists will share it). That is, his belief functions, or can function, as a premise in an argument. By con-trast, Wain's belief that the poor and outcast have human rights like the rest of us would be ludicrous if presented as a premise in an argument that John-son was a humane man. This shows that beliefs can ground other beliefs, contributing to the justness, objectivity, and certitude of the latter, without being premises for them.

We might remark, by the way, on an application of this insight to histor-ical judgments about Jesus (one that Climacus does not draw out). We have seen that a "subjective" qualification such as a belief in justice can render a person's assessment of another more "objective." Given that Johnson was actually the kind of man Wain depicts him to be, then it takes a person with certain moral traits to see this clearly, to appreciate Johnson for who he was, to sort the data in a fitting manner and to lay the emphases at the right places. Analogously, one might suggest, if Jesus is in fact the son of God, then it would not be surprising if the only people really qualified to make objective his-torical judgments about him were those with certain appropriate subjective qualifications, namely, the eyes and heart of faith. Critical Gospel scholar-ship in the last 150 years has thought it necessary, in the interest of histor-ical objectivity, to divorce historical work as much as possible from faith, and to depend instead upon techniques that can be equally well developed by persons with or without religious interests or sensitivities. (Such has been the ideology. The practice has been that of both believers and unbelievers riding their hobby horses across the texts.) It has been thought that the ap-ostolic writers were to be held historically suspect to the extent that they presented Jesus from the perspective of their faith in him. Such a supposi-tion is begging the question of Jesus' identity, for if he is who they claim he is, then their faith (in stark contrast with the historical critic's armory of techniques) subjectively qualifies them to be most objective about him. If Climacus is right, to hope that such exercise of generally acceptable tech-niques and premises might issue in the conclusion that Jesus is who the apostles say he is, is a hope doomed from the outset.

This, then, is the central insight of Climacus's Interlude: No historical personage (or indeed any event at all) is a flat, straightforward, self-inter-preting brute datum given to an unambiguous apprehension. Every histor-ical judgment, whether made by an eyewitness of the personage in question or by someone in a subsequent generation dependent on testimony, is shaped ultimately by a set of beliefs held by the individual making the judgment, which beliefs form a kind of interpretive mold out of which the judgment emerges, and in virtue of which the judgment is certified. If this were not so, two consequences of interest to Climacus would seem to follow.

First, eyewitnesses would be in an absolutely privileged position. There would be no such thing as an improvement of historical accounts by later noneyewitnesses, whose main contribution is not in the data they are able to collect, but in the way they construe the data they have. There would be no such thing as a biographer, two hundred years after the fact and with only documents to go on, understanding Johnson better than any of his contemporaries understood him. Nor would it be possible for the apostle Paul, looking back on the traditions that had been handed down to him concerning Jesus of Nazareth, to understand better his identity and significance than had most of those who walked with him in the days of his earthly sojourn. If, under the hypothesis that historical facts are brutes, reports of them were possible (and it is hard to see how they would be), the reports would have to be accepted simply "at face value." For such facts would have only faces, in the sense of surfaces; they would be without "depth."

Because historical judgments depend on belief-structures, that a judgment is based on "immediate cognition" rather than testimony affords it only a very weak and partial claim to epistemic superiority. Judgments made by persons possessing only testimony are often superior to ones made by the "eyewitnesses" with whom the testimony originated. In a paragraph in chapter five that is laden with the dialectical tension by which Climacus prevents the reader's appropriating what he says as a direct communication, he makes passing reference to this fact. He imagines someone who himself has never heard or seen Jesus, living in the generation when there are still eyewitnesses alive. This man has a historian's compulsion for learning all the details about Jesus, and possesses the power to arraign the witnesses and cross-examine them.

> If he managed to obtain a complicated report in agreement down to the letter and to the minute—then beyond all doubt he would be deceived. He would have attained a certainty even greater than that of the contemporary who saw and heard, for the latter would readily discover that he sometimes did not see and sometimes saw wrongly, and so also with his hearing. (93)[7]

[7]This truism is clearly at odds with Climacus's repeated claim that immediate cognitions and they alone are objectively unimpeachable. Indeed, this claim is reflected a little earlier in the paragraph from which I have just quoted. He says that while being acquainted with persons who have witnessed an event may seem an epistemic advantage, "it is no doubt deceptive, for the person who is not so close to

The second consequence of ignoring the role of "beliefs" in historical judgments is that we might posit a different kind of difference than in fact there is between ordinary historical judgments and Christian faith. Climacus stresses the peculiarity of faith as a species of historical judgment, but he wants to pinpoint the peculiarity accurately. It is not that faith is an interpretive garb, wrapped externally around some otherwise brute facts, like white tie and tails draped around a turkey—whereas the "objective" history recorded by historians is a neutral reporting of uninterpreted facts, a presentation of the sheerly unadorned turkey-in-itself. The presence of judgment, construal, construction, belief-foundation, or whatever you call it, in the Christian historical claim, does not differentiate it from any other historical judgment. In other words, Climacus is denying that there is the kind of epistemological difference between Christian faith and ordinary historical judgments that in the middle decades of this century many German theologians affirmed with their disjunction of *Geschichte* from *Historie*.

Instead, the peculiarity of Christian faith consists in the fact that "common sense" contains insufficient support beliefs to generate the judgment that Jesus of Nazareth is the son of God and the atonement for the sins of the world. Before the judgment is owned up to, persons beholding it from the vantage point of the various forms of common sense find it outrageous and insulting. To put the matter at its mildest, from the point of view of common sense (even, for example, that eligible common sense that can see in Samuel Johnson a liberal and humane man), it looks as though there is something much too hardy in the judgment that Jesus is the son of God. We frequently run into liberal and humane persons, and if we have some moral sensitivity we will normally recognize them with considerable certitude. It is entirely unclear, from this standpoint, what it would be to "recognize" somebody as the son of God. Ordinary forms of common sense do not contain the groundwork, the web, of beliefs that will certify this judgment. This is what Climacus means when he calls the fact that Jesus is the son of God "a fact based upon a self-contradiction" (87). There are clues, no doubt, indications that can be apprehended as signs by way of beliefs that are present in common sense. When Jesus says to the paralytic, "My son, your sins are

---

the immediate certainty that he is immediately certain is absolutely distanced" (91). On this principle our imagined historian is absolutely distanced from immediate certainty. It follows, then, that one who is absolutely separated from an immediate certainty may have "a certainty even greater than that of" one who was in possession of such an immediate certainty! You will agree that Climacus is quite a rascal. People looking for a doctrine to skim off the surface of the text will be disconcerted; and they will regain the concert of their minds only by pushing off from Climacus and thinking for themselves.

forgiven," the scribes sitting by judge that blasphemy is being committed, in virtue of the common sense that (1) this man is forgiving sins on his own authority, and (2) only God can forgive sins that way. Common sense can presumably judge that (1) he filled the stomachs of a big crowd, starting out with only five loaves and a couple of fish and (2) this is extraordinary. None of the beliefs that are present in the structure of common sense even come close to certifying the judgment to which these commonly apprehensible facts are clues, namely, that the historical Jesus is the eternal son of God. Because of our sin that belief, as Climacus reminds us repeatedly, must be received directly from the god himself, by a kind of intervention, a miracle. Or, in the more usual language of the church, the believer must receive the belief by an authoritative, first-hand testimony: the witness of the Holy Spirit.

As we have noted before, common sense is necessarily a relative notion, and when we say that common sense (or better, common senses) find the Christian judgment about Jesus strange and offensive, we are speaking, of course, of common sense as it exists unaided by this judgment. The recognition of Jesus is a personal meeting with God, a transformation of the self in the direction of holiness—of love for God and love for neighbor. To recognize Jesus is to recognize oneself, along with the rest of humankind, as the beloved of God, as having been drawn into his family by the blood of Christ. It is to tell the story (which might be told otherwise) with a twist that cannot be grounded in our ordinary beliefs about characters. So in faith one sees the world anew: one sees the beauty of persons more poignantly, they being the objects of God's great love; and the ugliness of evil more poignantly, it being the object of God's sorrow and displeasure. This new vision of life is grounded in a new creation of the minds of believers, produced by that testimony of the Holy Spirit.

CHAPTER 5

THE FOLLOWER
AT SECOND HAND

THE FINAL CHAPTER OF *FRAGMENTS* is a continuation of Climacus's exploration of the grammar of faith, this time with a focus on persons inhabiting
a generation whose only access to the history in question is through testimonies. His main point is that there is no advantage for acquiring faith, to
being a historical contemporary of the god in time, or closer to him in time.
Though faith is a historical judgment, Saint Peter is not privileged above Saint
Catherine of Siena, and neither is privileged above you and me.

Climacus divides his last chapter into two parts, between which there
arises a certain dialectical tension. The first part is a comparison of the first
generation of non-contemporary disciples with the generation that exists
1,843 years after the coming of the "teacher." The question is, What advantages and disadvantages belong to occupants of these two positions in history, with respect to the problem of becoming a believer? The second part
is a set of remarks ostensibly designed to explain why there is no such thing
as a "disciple at second hand." Those remarks do, in fact, afford the reader
an occasion for making sense of this grammatical remark. In chapter five, as
in others we have examined, Climacus mixes his elements so as to set up a
dialectical commotion that the careful reader will feel compelled to still. Not
everything he says here can be taken straightforwardly; it is a mixture of jest
and earnest by which the author slips away, leaving the reader on his own
to find and own the truth.

THE JOLTING IMPACT
OF OUR FACT

The first and last generations of non-contemporary disciples each possess a peculiar "advantage." The first is "closer to the jolt" (93) of our fact.
So the first generation has some safeguard against underestimating the difficulty of coming to faith; since they feel the "terror" (99) involved in confronting this lowly man who gives signs of being their God, they have a clear
idea of what they are up against. The advantage of Climacus's own generation, in 1843, is that it can look at all the magnificent historical achieve-
ments of Christianity—the phenomenal spread of the church, the imbuing

of whole cultures with "Christian values," the preservation and establishment of learning in the West, and so forth. From this synoptic vantage point
it can see how probable it is that Christianity is true. Surrounded on all sides
by the fruits of Christianity, it seems hardly possible for a sane person to
have any objection to it.

Climacus's grouping of these two resources under the rubric of advantages is clearly ironical. To feel the jolt and the terror that the original disciples felt when presented with the paradoxical claim that this humble,
suffering servant was God himself—this is a genuine advantage. True, it is
"completely dialectical," (93) since it is possible that the confrontation will
issue in the unhappy relationship of offense rather than the happy one of
faith. Still, "the advantage is that one enters into a state in which the decision manifests itself ever more clearly" (93). By contrast, the "advantage of
ease" (99) that the later generation enjoys by virtue of having naturalized or
deparadoxicalized the historical fact in question is not, from the standpoint
of faith, an advantage in any sense. It is pure danger. The person lounging
in the cozy comfort of this cultural deception does not even have the possibility of coming to faith. He is as far from faith as the aborigine who has
never heard the gospel. No, he is even farther away, for if the aborigine heard
the gospel clearly preached, he might grasp the news with the appropriate
awe. But he who rests his belief in Jesus on the consequences of the Christian movement, and thus naturalizes Jesus into a cultural phenomenon, is
inoculated against a primitive grasp of the claim.

> If it were to occur to the latest generation, observing the first generation and
> seeing it almost collapsing under the terror, to say, "This is inconceivable, for
> the whole thing is not so heavy that one cannot pick it up and run with it"—
> there no doubt would be someone who would reply, "Please, why do you not
> run with it; but just be sure that what you are running with is actually what is
> under discussion. We certainly do not dispute the fact that it is easy enough
> to run with the wind. (98-99)

Climacus clearly believes that a lively sense of the jolt produced by the
teacher's claim is an advantage from the perspective of faith, dialectical
though it be. One of the most important purposes of the expression "absolute paradox" is to remind the reader how shocking and unnaturalizable this
claim is. Anyone who accepts it without feeling the shock has not understood it.

There are a number of ways the jolt may be cushioned. One is reinterpretation. What does it mean to say that this man is God? Climacus objects
to the Hegelian domestication of the claim, which goes something like this:
The dialectical "moment" centering around Jesus of Nazareth was a major
step in the realization of Absolute Spirit, which is the realization of the unity
of the divine and the human. Had Climacus lived a hundred years later, he

certainly would have objected as well to the existentialist reinterpretation: Somehow in Jesus the disciples (and we) encounter the demand and the possibility of living our daily finite lives by the resource of the infinite, the Wholly Other, the Radically Transcendent, the Nothingness on the other side of finite being. This Nothingness is what has traditionally been called "God." So in the man Jesus we encounter God. Such reinterpretations make Jesus' claim over into something less jolting, with far less potential to offend. To call such a Jesus the absolute paradox would be extravagant hyperbole.

Another method of domesticating Jesus, often used in tandem with reinterpretation, is historical denial and reconstruction. One simply denies that Jesus claimed to be God, and then explains away the Gospels' claim that he made such a claim by some theory about the development of ideas in early Christianity. Jesus was a simple moral and religious teacher, said some nineteenth-century liberals, who never claimed anything so extreme as that he was the son of God; it was Paul and other early theologians who committed this outrage. More recently, the tendency is to say that Jesus was an apocalyptic preacher of the kingdom of God, but certainly did not claim to be God himself. To explain why the New Testament says he did, one must suppose the existence of congregations in very early Christianity, with membership composed of people coming out of pagan religious traditions in which there was no hesitation (as there would have been in straight Jewish congregations) to ascribe divinity to a man. It was in these churches that the notion grew up that Jesus was the Lord and son of God in the sense that he himself *was* God. From them it spread to the larger Christian community.[1]

Now if I am convinced that Jesus in no way claimed to be God, and that this claim on his behalf was fabricated by people who were ignorant or superstitious or prone to invent myths, then I will find nothing jolting about the story. I may be surprised by what the primitive mind was capable of, or shocked by Paul's lack of intellectual integrity, or amused by the stupidity of the apostles, but I shall be inoculated forever against the shock of which Climacus speaks. His account of the jolt, and of the relative advantage of being close to the contemporary generation, presupposes that the historical de-

---

[1]See for example Werner Georg Kümmel, *The Theology of the New Testament* (Nashville and New York: Abingdon Press, 1973) ch. 2. As to the evidential basis of this hypothesis, Kümmel is more candid than most of its exponents: "But we have as few direct sources for Hellenistic-Jewish and Hellenistic-Gentile Christianity as for the Palestinian primitive community; therefore the forms of belief of these preliminary stages of the later Gentile-Christian primitive Christianity cannot be put forth except as hypothetical" (119). And just how many direct sources for the Palestinian primitive community do we have? "We do not have any sources which will allow us a direct look into the preaching and the faith of the primitive community" (105).

nials and reconstructions are false. Consequently, against a generation prone to accept such denials and reconstructions (and thus to gird itself against the possibility of faith) Climacus's suppositions would imply that the debunking of such scholarship is an essential part of rousing dull spirits to appreciate the shock of the Christian gospel. Such a procedure might be just as important as the conceptual clarification that he effects by the concept of absolute paradox. A person might fear that by venturing into this vast and muddy field he will get bogged down in the endless details of ancient literature and the swarming subtleties of historical argument. Not necessarily. No more would be needed than to take the few paradigm theories of the development of the idea that Jesus was God, and to show how speculative and arbitrary they are, and how based on poor literary judgment. For an indication of what can be achieved by a few simple but masterful thrusts at the vital organs of skeptical historical reconstruction, I recommend C. S. Lewis's address, "Modern Theology and Biblical Criticism."[2]

The point is that by emphasizing the importance for all potential believers of feeling the jolt that Jesus' contemporaries felt, Climacus implied the importance to Christian faith of certain minimal beliefs that are historical in the ordinary sense: If we believe that Jesus gave no "sign" that he was God incarnate, then the claim that he is has about as much shocking force for us as the assertion that Julius Caesar was God.

THE UNIMPORTANCE
OF THE HISTORICAL DETAIL

There is a certain dialectical tension between sections one and two of chapter five. The grammatical remark on which section two centers, and in which Climacus climaxes *Fragments,* is "There is no follower [that is, disciple] at second hand" (104). Climacus wants to present this idea starkly and forcefully, to incite his reader by the extremity of his formulations first to take notice and then to think his way to an inflected understanding of the grammar of faith. Some passages in this latter section, if cited in isolation from the previous section, give the clear impression that equality between the generations of disciples requires that faith bear no grammatical connection with any ordinary historical beliefs: that somehow, one can believe that God has become a particular man who lived at a particular time in history, without believing anything else to be true of him. To stop with this impression is to misinterpret these passages. The tension between stressing the "jolt" and severing the connection between ordinary history and the absolute paradox demands *some* resolution, and it would be unreasonable to

---

[2]Walter Hooper, ed., *Christian Reflections,* (Grand Rapids MI: Wm. B. Eerdmans Publishing Company, 1967) 152ff.

resolve it by treating as unserious Climacus's comments about preserving the "jolt" connected with the signs.

Climacus begins by presenting "a few observations for orientation" (99) before addressing directly the question of how the testimony of others figures in the faith of a non-contemporary disciple. (A) "If that fact is regarded as a simple historical fact, then being contemporary counts for something. . . . Every historical fact is only a relative fact, and therefore it is entirely appropriate for the relative power, time, to decide the relative fates of people with respect to contemporaneity" (99). (B) If the fact in question is an eternal truth, "then every age is equally close to it" (99). (C) "If that fact . . . is what we have set forth, then it is a contradiction for time to be able to apportion the relations of people to it" (99).

Let me comment on each of these remarks. When it comes to simple historical facts, what makes contemporaneity "count for something"? As we saw in the last two sections of our comments on the Interlude, access to "immediate cognitions" does not guarantee, or even render the probability high, that the historical judgments built on them will be either more certain or more penetrating than judgments built on reports of such cognitions. Since contemporaneity normally carries with it as many epistemic liabilities (for example, narrowness of vision, lack of a body of developed reflection about the fact in question) as advantages, it would not seem to be an *epistemic* desideratum. A person who thought it was would probably be victim of the delusion that, had *he* been a contemporary, he would have had the penetrating questions and framework for *understanding* what he would see with his eyes, which he now has only in virtue of belonging to a later generation.

I think Climacus has in mind an *aesthetic* advantage that attends contemporaneity. He admits that there is a kind of "magnificence" that can be appreciated much more richly in person than through the mediation of any possible account: the marriage festivities of an emperor, for example, involving beauties to the eyes, ears, nostrils, and palate (see 66-67). And perhaps more generally it is allowable that we take a kind of curious interest, an interest of the eyes and ears, even a nosy interest, as it were, in "simple historical facts." There is nothing wrong with reading a biography of Samuel Johnson out of nothing more than curiosity about what the great man was like. But having read about Johnson, who would not love to have just a peek at him? What a delight to witness his lumbering gait, his sonorous voice, the twinkle in his squinting eye as he talked. As a weak substitute for such impossible experiences, Johnson enthusiasts make pilgrimages to his habitations, fondle his inkwells, delight in the discovery of new trivia about him, and seek an ever more detailed and minutely accurate account. People may yearn to hear the sound of Johnson's voice, Climacus is saying, but since only something relative (aesthetic) is here at stake, there is nothing unfitting about time, the relative power, saying to such people "Tough luck, you are forever debarred from satisfaction."

Climacus's deeper point, however, is contrastive: Such a curiosity is entirely improper with respect to Jesus Christ. To be interested in his mannerisms, the pitch of his voice, the texture of his skin, the exact chronology of his ministry, the number and detail of his miracles, and so forth, is to be distracted from the momentous issue at hand, namely whether you will own him as your Lord and savior. To adopt the historian's attitude toward Jesus that many Johnson enthusiasts take toward Johnson, is a kind of blasphemy. Climacus makes reference to the words of Jesus' farewell to his disciples, "Nevertheless I tell you the truth: it is for your good that I am leaving you" (John 16:7; see 105). He interprets them to mean it is better that such curiosity be forcibly starved, that disciples be not led into this temptation.

Little needs to be said about Climacus's second comment. While it is possibly true that "every age is equally close" to eternal truths, not every individual is equally near them. If that were so, there would seem to be no need for Socratic teachers; for it seems a matter of fact that some people would never come to the insights of Socratic religion if some teacher did not come along. The individual's actually having the insight is in that case a consequence of the historical presence of his teacher. Of course Climacus's point is again contrastive: Christian faith differs from the Socratic religion of generally available insights, to which people may need to be stimulated; for faith is the belief that the coming into the world of a particular individual is the redemption of the world, and so coming to faith requires not just stimulation to insight, but information that the event has happened.

Climacus's third remark, that "it is a contradiction for time to be able to apportion the relations of people to" the redemption accomplished by the coming of Jesus Christ into the world, "that is, . . . in a crucial sense," (125) seems to suggest that the justice of God is inconsistent with his allowing an individual's eternal salvation to hang on whether he has faith during this life. For if a person cannot have faith without receiving certain historical information, then those who are not in a position to get this information cannot have faith. There have certainly been many people in the history of the world who had no access to this information. If salvation depends on faith, and if Climacus is right about the justice of God, then people must be given opportunities for faith beyond the limits of the present life.

It seems to me that such a conclusion is consistent with Climacus's central tenets. He asks how "an eternal happiness [can] be built on historical knowledge" (see the title page), and what he says about this will fit a North American aborigine who lived in the year 8,000 B.C. as well as anybody else. An eternal happiness is based on historical knowledge when (1) the knowledge in question is the message that Jesus has lived and died among us for the redemption of the recipient of the knowledge, (2) the recipient has this information imparted to him, and (3) God grants the condition on which the consciousness of the recipient is transformed by this information into a happy God-relationship. The only peculiarity of the aborigine's case is that (2) occurs in another existence than the one in which you and I have received this information.

However, Climacus's inquiry obviously does not have this kind of case primarily in mind, but instead the case of you and me, who get the requisite information in this life all right, but get it in the form of testimony from others. His point is: Because of our "accidental" positioning in space and time, Saint Peter and I differ in the way we get this information. I rely wholly on testimony for it, whereas he got it with minimal reliance on testimony. This difference, just by itself, however, does not differentiate me from Peter as to the potential for certainty, profundity, and primitivity of faith.

Climacus does not mean to deny that "accidents" of history can erect special obstacles to faith. He interprets a passage from John's Gospel as suggesting that Jesus' physical presence was a potential obstacle to faith, an obstacle with which Peter had to contend, but not you and I. He believes that Christianity can be rendered less accessible by confusions that pollute the intellectual air—like those perpetrated by well-meaning apologists who "naturalize" the absolute paradox, or by the reinterpretations of Hegelian or Heideggerian theologians, or even, it seems, by certain historical hypotheses that can gain currency. These are obstacles with which Climacus and we, because of our placement in space and time, have to contend. It is a major purpose of his books to dismantle such historically accidental hurdles to faith.

The irony of the three remarks on which I have just commented, if they are indeed ironical, is a gentle one. Each of them can easily mislead an undialectical or lazy mind. They call out to the reader to interpret and qualify them as I have done; they beckon him to reflection. The irony of the remarks on which I now wish to comment is much starker. Here even a fairly casual reader is likely to feel his mind abused and spurred to cast about for resolution.

Climacus asks, *"What, then, can a contemporary do for someone who comes later?"* and answers that there are two things he can do: "(a) He can tell someone who comes later that he himself has believed that fact," while emphasizing that "it is folly to the understanding and an offense to the human heart;" and "(b) In this form he can tell the content of the fact, a content that still is only for faith, in quite the same sense as colors are only for sight and sound for hearing" (102). What is interesting (and incensing) about this paragraph is that it leaves out entirely the sort of thing that the contemporary witnesses to Jesus in fact did for their successors, the sort of thing that occupies almost the entirety of the four Gospels. These do not merely testify to belief and relate a content that "exists only for faith." They tell the story of this man's life in such a way that it becomes evident why someone might pick *him* out of the millions and say that he is the son of God and the lamb that takes away the sins of the world. They recount numerous incidents that existed for people without faith, namely the many things that he publicly did and said and underwent. In other words they convey the "fact" in such a way as to give an impression of the "jolt" it produced, and in such a way as to render understandable the "terror" under which the contemporary generation labored, and under which any subsequent generation must also labor if it is to relate itself with fitting pathos to this fact. It is impossible to think Climacus means us to take at face value what he says here.

Climacus continues, "The heart of the matter is the historical fact that the god has been in human form, and the other historical details are not even as important as they would be if the subject were a human being instead of the god" (103-104). Here Climacus's use of the expression "the other historical details" is surely intended comically. It is a "grammatical joke" or an amusing category mistake, as when one says, "She arrived in a flood of tears and a sedan chair," or "This book contains 350 pages, twelve color photographs, and five ideas." It is as though the fact that this man is God is *one* historical detail, which is "the essence of the matter," and everything else— his discussion of the law, his parables, his ministry to the poor and suffering, his forgiving of sins and healing of diseases, his bloody death and glorious resurrection—is "the *other* historical details," which are even less important here than the details of, say, Samuel Johnson's life. It is no doubt true that these details have importance for faith only as they are indications of Jesus' identity and mission. So faith is not interested in how tall Jesus was, how often he washed his hair, and whether he had impaired eyesight, because such details would not function as signs of his identity. That Jesus is the son of God is not one historical detail alongside many others in his biography, any more than the ideas in a book are "in" it in the same sense as the pages and the photographs are "in" it. That Jesus is Lord is rather a truth that we come to by construing some of the details of his biography, by taking them as clues to who he is. Faith is one way of making sense of the selection of details offered us in the Gospels. If we discarded all such details, faith would have nothing appropriate to make sense of.

I want to conclude this section by commenting on a passage that is surely the starkest statement in this section of chapter five of the thesis that all historical detail is inessential for faith:

> Even if the contemporary generation had not left anything behind except these words, "We have believed that in such and such a year the god appeared in the humble form of a servant, lived and taught among us, and then died"—

this is more than enough. The contemporary generation would have done what is needful, for this little announcement, this world-historical *nota bene,* is enough to become an occasion for someone who comes later, and the most prolix report can never in all eternity become more for the person who comes later. (104)

To feel the irony we need only use our imagination. Represent to yourself someone in a library reading room, otherwise entirely uninformed about this event, coming across this announcement on page 693 in volume three of a book of universal history. I think we can predict that such a *nota bene* would not be sufficient to afford an occasion for this reader to become a new creation. One would predict that he will read such a passage mildly amused, then wonder for a moment whether the source of this testimony was joking, deranged, or in the grip of some pagan cult. He will then turn unjolted to page 694. As a Christian one might say, "Well, I suppose God *might* have elected to transform people by such a rootless, thin, and ambiguous testimony. With him all things are possible. But that is not how the Holy Spirit usually works. In the beginning he tied his work to the more or less public activities of Jesus; these days, he ties it to the scriptural witness."

CONCLUDING REMARKS

It is no overstatement to say that Climacus has avoided a "doctrinizing" presentation of the grammatical connections between believing testimonies and having faith. By juxtaposing his emphasis on the importance of the "jolt" of God's incarnation against the kind of remarks that we have just examined, he effectively cuts the reader loose from his mooring in the text, and sends him off to navigate these waters for himself. Of course the reader is not left entirely to his own devices, for like any good Socratic teacher Climacus has supplied him with hints that will aid him, if he perseveres, to make his own way home. In this final section I want to sketch roughly what I take to be the right way to blend the various hints that Climacus has provided into a coherent account of this aspect of the grammar of faith.

Climacus's thesis is that there is no disciple at second hand. By this he means to deny that those who walked with Jesus have any advantage, respecting the quality of their faith, over those who must depend on historical testimonies. It is perhaps useful to focus here on one quality of faith in which the original disciples might be thought to have an advantage, namely certainty. Saint Peter's faith, for example, seems to be consequential, in part, upon his having seen Jesus alive after his death. Saint Catherine of Siena's faith, by contrast, is partially consequential upon her acceptance of the testimony of Peter and others that they saw Jesus alive after his death. Now surely, one will say, Peter's faith is for this reason of higher quality—that is, a greater certainty—than Catherine's. In response to this challenge, let us ask the obvious question: Is Catherine in fact less certain that Jesus is the son of God than Peter? The answer is that we have no reason to think so. Climacus's thesis seems to be borne out by the facts: In every age, and not just in the first century, we find intelligent people who are completely convinced that Jesus is the son of God.

Our interest here is not sociological, but grammatical. So we would like to see what grammatical or logical features Christian faith has that enable it to be true that there is no disciple at second hand. Because in general historical judgments hang in belief-structures, it is not necessarily true that an eyewitness of a historical event is more certain of the occurrence and character of it than another individual who knows of it only through testimony. Indeed, Peter's certainty that he had seen the risen Lord may very well have been increased by hearing the testimony of others as to appearances that he did not witness. Catherine, having the reflection and information of the entire New Testament available to her, had resources for historical certainty that Peter may have lacked. (He of course may have had sources that she lacked, too.) So a kind of rough potential equality may exist between eyewitnesses and non-eyewitnesses, due to the belief-dependency of historical judgments.

Of course faith is not the belief that Jesus was raised from the dead, or that he did certain miracles, or said certain things. It is the belief that he is God incarnate reconciling the sinner to himself; and consequently it is a reconstrual of oneself and the entire world with such profound attitudinal and behavioral corollaries that the believer can be called a new creation. The historical judgment that is faith appropriately comes to occupy a central and determining position in the consciousness of the believer. It becomes the judgment upon which all his judgments about himself, his fellow human beings, and his attitudes toward the natural world, pivot: Who is he? One redeemed and commissioned by Jesus Christ. Who are his fellows? Brothers and sisters, or at least potentially such, redeemed like him and granted membership in the household of God. What are the earth and the stars, the trees and lakes and animals? They are the handiwork of the father of Jesus Christ, to whom reverence and praise are due on their account. So this historical judgment begins to occupy a place in the believer's view of reality as a whole that is analogous to the place that the machinist's belief in his calipers occupies in relation to all his activities around the machine shop. The belief shapes and determines, makes possible, all his activities and attitudes.

In a way, too, it comes to be borne out by all those activities and attitudes. Ask a mature believer what it would be like for him to give up the belief that Jesus is the son of God and redeemer, and you will hear words like "despair," "my life would fall apart," "to whom would I turn?" The belief in Jesus becomes a certainty not by being deducible from irrefragable premises, or inferable with probability from the "signs," but by virtue of the place that it comes to occupy in a person's life. It is the focus of the sinner's fellowship with God, and is consequently conceived by the believer as a miraculous performance of God. It can occupy that place because there is something deeply fitting about it, fitting to the human heart, at the same time as, and partly because, it is repelling to common sense.

We have also seen that the judgment that Jesus is the redeemer would be absurd in a way inadmissible to Climacus, if the believer disbelieved that certain "ordinary" historical events—events "visible" to nonbelievers—did not occur. Persons who scrutinize the testimonies to most ordinary events will assign them one or another degree of probability, depending on what other things the individual believes. I do not deny that beliefs concerning Jesus' "signs" are subject, in principle, to a like ambivalence; but in the present case such ambivalence is highly unstable. If you are inclined to be offended at the claim, you will tend to deny that the claim is real—by historical reconstruction, by reinterpretation, or even by claiming that Jesus is mad or devilish (see Mark 3). On the other hand, if you are inclined toward faith, you will tend to settle into a firm conviction that the signs are, on the whole, historical. By becoming one of the assumptions of one's life-view (the life-view that pivots on the judgment that Jesus is the Lord and savior of the world), this conviction gets a derivative firmness.

But, you may say, such a firm conviction is irrational, possibly even immoral. To treat a set of ordinary historical events as a collective certainty, when it has at most a high degree of probability, is to violate the rules of historical research, and to be intellectually irresponsible. Well, I admit that it may be to *ignore* the rules of historical research; but surely it would not be to *violate* them unless one were doing historical research, which the believer as believer is decidedly not doing. But if he is not violating any rules, then the charges of immorality and irresponsibility are misplaced. If the believer engages in historical research on this matter, then of course, *for the purposes of that research,* he will not treat these events as a certainty. For example, if asked how probable they are on historical grounds, he will measure his judgment in the way that historians do, and his answer will certainly not be, one hundred percent. But that does not mean that he will then measure the conduct of his life in general (for example, his worship of God, the religious education of his children, the rejoicing in his salvation) to a probability of less than one hundred percent.

In accusing the believer of irresponsibility you may be thinking of something like this. Imagine Saint Catherine going about her life in Siena. That Jesus is God is beyond doubt for her; and that he claimed to be such is equally beyond doubt. Now Rudolf Bultmann, by some miracle, appears at the University of Siena, lecturing on the synoptic tradition and proclaiming it as an assured result of modern scholarship that none of the "signs" are historical. He bases his claim on the hypothesis of the Hellenistic communities in early Christianity, but refrains from informing his audience that he has no evidence for this hypothesis. Saint Catherine listens dutifully to the great professor, and of course is unaware of his intellectual sleight-of-hand. Is she irresponsible and irrational if she continues in her devotion to Jesus? Not, surely, unless she believes that the signs are all unhistorical. And why should she believe that? Just because a German professor tells her so? You and I know that Bultmann is whistling in the dark, and so we have a powerful source of skepticism with which to meet his skepticism. But one of the glorious things about Catherine's faith is that it too is a source of skepticism: Having lived in intimate fellowship with her Lord these many years, having experienced his kindness and mercy, having been made a new creation through faith in him, what is she to say to a lecture like Bultmann's? She will be puzzled, no doubt, but her doubts will probably all go one way: "Poor man, I wonder where he went wrong."

Perhaps you will want to press this question: How probable, on purely historical grounds, does it have to be that the signs are historical for it not to be irrational for a person to affirm that Jesus is the son of God? Imagine that I am hanging on a piece of sage-brush over a three-thousand-foot chasm. Fifteen feet below is a ledge from which I can climb to safety, but it is about six feet laterally from me. If I let go straight down I shall fall 3000 feet; if I can get my body swinging and then let go at just the right moment, I may land on that ledge. Now how probable does it have to be that the sage will hold through this operation, that I will have the strength and skill to let go at just the right moment, and so forth, for it not to be irrational for me to give it a try? The answer is obvious: It does not have to be very probable. Surely I shall be demoralized if I think the probability of success is zero. But if I perceive even a little probability, and am courageous, I shall be able to give myself whole-heartedly to the project, and nobody will accuse me of irrationality because of the slim prospect of success. As Climacus remarks in another book, "Christianity was also a desperate way out when it first came into the world, and in all ages remains such; because it is a desperate way out for everyone who really accepts it" (*Postscript,* 96). With respect to sin and death we are all like the fellow hanging over the chasm; we are not in a position to wait around bargaining for a salvation whose probability better suits our fancy. In saying this I am not admitting that the probability of the signs' being historical is low. I am only saying that I would not *have* to consider it very high for it to be rational for me to make the belief in Jesus focal in the way the Christian does.

Most simple believers, upon hearing the gospel preached, probably do not even reflect on the probability of the signs' being historical. They just accept the assumption. If they have a little sophistication, there are two considerations that may cause them to assess this probability, and possibly to assess it as rather low. Some will have heard that modern science tells us that the world is a seamless weave of cause and effect, and that events like walking on water, multiplying loaves, miraculous healings, and resurrection from the dead, are thus shown *a priori* to be impossible. So we do not even need to do any historical research to know that many of the signs—namely all those involving a miraculous element—are unhistorical. But it is not true that modern science tells us about this seamless weave. It no doubt usually assumes, for its own purposes, that there will be no break with the usual patterns of events. But individual scientists, all of whom perhaps make this assumption in their scientific work, would differ as to whether to apply the assumption across the board. Whether they do or not is not a result of their science, but of their metaphysics; both the assumption that the patterns are inviolable and the refusal to make this assumption across the board, are matters of belief, and which belief one adopts is left open by scientific research.

The other consideration that may lead a believer to assess as low the probability of the signs' being historical is the presence of the radical historical reconstructions. It is perhaps worth reflecting in this connection that no radical hypothesis has the intrinsic probability that the straightforward historical claims of the biblical text have. Over the past two hundred years or so, radical hypotheses have swarmed in profusion, one after another blossoming into favor only to be scorned by another school or to go out of style in the succeeding generation. An ignorant person who hears a hypothesis like that of Schonfield's *Passover Plot* presented with a straight face may be deeply hurt by it, since in his poverty of perspective he may take it to be the simple and obvious truth. Similarly a biblical scholar who has been intimidated by his mentors or seduced by a reigning fashion may take the passing hypothesis of the day as an "assured result of scholarship." But all of this is foolishness and myopia. A perspective on the past couple of centuries of biblical scholarship ought to beget a certain skeptical wisdom: the vision of thousands of highly intelligent, industrious, and learned people, using what seem to be the most sophisticated scholarly techniques of their day, focusing all their brilliance on a tiny set of ancient documents—having utterly failed to show that the signs are unhistorical. This vision does not, of course, prove that the signs *are* historical; but it does establish that as of today, a person who believes that these events, or some suitably similar ones, occurred, is well within his epistemic rights.

* * * * *

Climacus is that rare combination, dialectician *and* poet. It is his conviction that Christianity, in being an affair of the heart (faith is a "happy passion"), is a matter of the mind (the happy passion has a "dialectic," a logic—what I have called its "grammar"). The importance of the *Fragments* project derives from the fact that to get this grammar wrong is not just an intellectual mishap, like holding an inconsistent economic theory or believing falsehoods about Napoleon. It is a distortion of thought that reverberates through the entire personality, affecting the spirit itself, the passions concerning one's value and identity as a person, the meaning of one's activities, and one's relationship with God. Since the problem of becoming a Christian is "pathetic-dialectic" (see *Postscript,* 493), the thinker who addresses grammatical distortions must combine the powers of an informal logician, a spiritually qualified depth-psychologist, and a religious "poet." As if this job description were not demanding enough, Climacus warns that, in the situation of Christendom, decisively Christian discourse will fall on deaf ears if it is presented directly; hence what is said must be sufficiently roundabout to make the reader reduplicate the thoughts—that is, rethink them after Climacus under the reader's own steam. So in a sense the reader has to become a poet-dialectician himself—or that is, at least, the tall order that Climacus's writings issue.

Surveying the literature about Climacus's literature, it has seemed to me that the overwhelming majority of it is out of step with his purpose. It is not *reading,* in the sense that would be invited by Climacus's understanding of his authorship. Most of it, indeed, is nothing but "Kierkegaard-scholarship," highly general and lacking both fine-grained dialectical analysis and poetical sensitivity. I have taken a small but central fragment of Climacus's literature and tried, in my poor way, to meet his challenge. I have tried to think Climacus's thoughts after him, to reduplicate in the sphere of thought, if not of existence, the adventure of *Philosophical Fragments.* This, it seems to me, and nothing less than this, is the kind of reading the book demands. *Fragments* is, by its author's intention, a very dark book, and one that occasions humility in its interpreter. As I have repeated throughout the body of this work, I am neither very confident, nor very concerned, that my thoughts actually reproduce those of Johannes Climacus (who is, after all, a figment). They are offered as what occurred to one man's mind as he read the text.

INDEX